THE
AMERICA
GROUND
HASTINGS

THE
AMERICA
GROUND
HASTINGS

STEVE PEAK

The History Press

Front cover image: The America Ground in 1811.
Back cover image: The old brig Noah's Ark, *converted into a home.*
(Hastings Museum)

First published 2021

The History Press
97 St George's Place,
Cheltenham,
Gloucestershire,
GL50 3QB
www.thehistorypress.co.uk

British Library Cataloguing in Publication Data.
A catalogue record for this book is available from the British Library.

ISBN 978 0 7509 9731 7

Typesetting and origination by Typo•glyphix, Burton-on-Trent
Printed in Turkey by Imak

CONTENTS

ACKNOWLEDGEMENTS

The three people who gave me the most help with this book are unfortunately no longer with us: Barry Funnell, Ion Castro and Davd Padgham. I helped Barry when he was researching and writing his large pamphlet *The America Ground*, published in 1989, the first and only reliable history of the America Ground to date. Shortly before Barry died, he offered to help me produce another history of the America Ground by drawing on new material that had come to light since 1989. He also passed on to me copies of many of his pictures and documents, as did my friends and local historians Ion and David when I told them what I was hoping to do. Both have since died.

Also giving me very useful help have been Ken Brooks, Denis Collins, Professor Fred Gray, Bob Hart, Brian Lawes, Bill Montgomery and Ian Shiner, plus the Hastings Reference Library (especially Gill Newman), Hastings Museum and Art Gallery, The Keep at Falmer and the Old Hastings Preservation Society.

I am a retired journalist and writer/publisher, and have spent most of my life in Hastings. I have written several local history books, including *Fishermen of Hastings* (first published in 1985), *A Pier Without Peer* (on the history of the Hastings and St Leonards piers) and *Mugsborough Revisited* (describing the local background to Robert Tressell's famous novel *The Ragged Trousered Philanthropists*, which was set in Hastings and St Leonards). I am the honorary curator of the Hastings Fishermen's Museum, and have been on Hastings Council's Museum Committee for over 30 years.

Steve Peak, 2021

IMAGE CREDITS

Many of the pictures in this book come from a collection put together by the author over many years, including the generous donations from the archives of Barry Funnell, Ion Castro and David Padgham. The pictures that do not come from that multi-person collection have been kindly loaned by the following people and organisations:

Hastings Museum   20 22 24 28 29 32 34 39 44 (both) 47 50 52 55 (both) 62 75 77 89 96 101 (right) 107 (top) 138 back cover

Hastings Reference
Library   8 21 30 94 101 (left) 113 123 139

The Keep,
Brighton   59 84

British Museum   73

Ken Brooks   80 (left)

Ordnance Survey   10

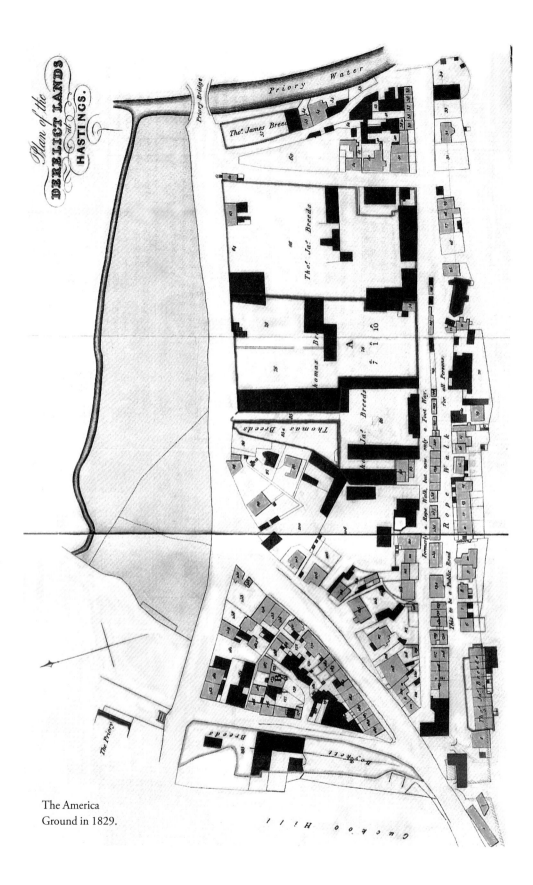

The America
Ground in 1829.

INTRODUCTION

The 'America Ground' is 8½ acres of Hastings town centre that in the early nineteenth century was an open piece of beach, apparently beyond the borough boundary and with no obvious owner, which was gradually occupied by a thousand or more people (many of them squatters) who lived and worked there – until they were all evicted by the government in 1835.

But in the first three decades of the nineteenth century, the Ground – despite being 'out of town' – played a key role in the expansion of Hastings during a crucial period in its 1,200-year history. The Ground was a combined industrial and housing estate providing many services to the town's developers, plus much housing for the many workers that were needed. The Ground's seeming freedom from local authority control also created something of a radical libertarian atmosphere, and one of the names the Ground acquired was 'America', after the newly independent former British colony.

However, the Ground's apparently almost uncontrolled sovereignty meant there was often conflict between the actual occupants as they tried to settle which of them was going to occupy what piece of landlord-free land. The increasing frequency of these clashes eventually prompted central government – the probable legal owner of the Ground – to take control of it in 1828. All the settlers were given notice to quit, and from 1850 what was once almost a new American state on British soil became an upmarket suburb of the increasingly popular seaside resort of Hastings.

There follows a summary of the America Ground's history, all of which is described in more detail in the rest of this book.

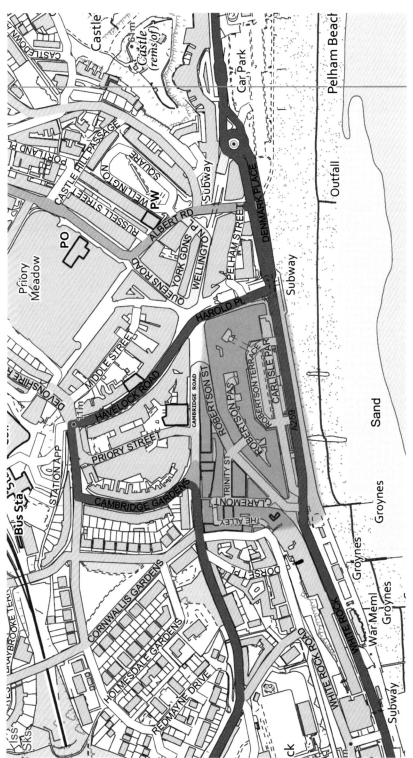

Hastings town centre. The America Ground was the coloured area, between Harold Place in the east and The Alley in the west, going as far inland as Cambridge Road.

SUMMARY

The America Ground lies in the Priory Valley, which around the time of the Battle of Hastings in 1066 was a natural harbour, with the town of Hastings then based on top of the White Rock headland, on the west side of the Valley. Over the following centuries the harbour gradually silted up, and Hastings moved into the Bourne Valley, where the Old Town is today.

In 1578 some prominent local townspeople persuaded Queen Elizabeth to fund the turning of the marshy Priory Valley into a 'haven', a sheltered closed-in dock, like a marina. But after £2,000 (about £920,000 in today's money) had been spent on the scheme in about 1580, the rest of the finance went missing and construction stopped. However, a raised embankment had been built across most of the mouth of the Valley from the west side, lying roughly where Cambridge Road is today, as a barrier providing defence from the sea. This embankment immediately created a valuable road out of Hastings to the west, and as such was also to become the inland boundary of the America Ground two centuries later.

But the embankment also blocked some of the Valley's drainage channels, turning the bottom of it into marshland. This had a major effect on the expansion of the town, as the Valley could not be built upon until the mid-nineteenth century.

By the early 1700s the Priory Valley had become a mixture of this low-lying marsh, with farmland on the slopes, and much shingle piled up against the c.1580 embankment. The Priory Stream ran down the east side of the Valley into the sea where Harold Place is now.

Then, in the 1790s, what had been the small fishing port of Hastings for the past two centuries started becoming a popular seaside resort, and much development began in the early 1800s. As the town could not expand to the east, it started spreading west under the Castle Cliff and into the Priory Valley, going as far as the Priory Stream. On the other side of the Stream were the marshes inland of the embankment, too wet to build on, while south of the embankment were the mostly unused acres of what was to become the America Ground. At that time it was usually known as the Priory Ground, named after the priory that had stood in the Valley from around 1190 until 1417, and which had owned much of it.

At the end of the eighteenth century the roads linking Hastings with London and elsewhere were poor quality, so the town was heavily dependent on seagoing vessels to transport people and goods. In 1800 the leading local shipowners, the Breeds family, took over a large part of the Priory Ground and built on it a 150yd-long ropewalk, for making the extended rope that was essential to all sailing craft, plus storage warehouses and workshops. It is believed that they arranged a lease for the land with the Earl of Chichester, who it was thought (wrongly, it transpired) to be the owner of the Ground.

BOOMTOWN

The expansion of Hastings speeded up from 1814, and work started in 1816 on building upmarket housing in Wellington Square and Castle Street, followed in 1820 by Pelham Place, and then Pelham Crescent from 1823. All this construction work on the east side of the Stream needed many labourers, skilled workers, workshops and stores, and as there were few available places in the existing town, the handy Priory Ground west of the Stream started becoming both a housing and industrial estate.

By 1820 the boom had accelerated, and the need for somewhere to live became especially urgent. At around that time it became clear that Hastings Corporation was not exercising any local authority rights it might have had over the Priory Ground, and, as the possible landlord, the Earl of Chichester, had a low public profile, people began squatting unchallenged on the Ground.

As the Ground appeared to be lying outside the town's border and had no clear landlord, so its residents and businesses had no taxes and little (if any) rent to pay. This meant that the financial overheads of running a trade or living there were low, while at the same time their employers could pay them less than usual, giving the developers more to invest – a mutually beneficial arrangement.

The Priory Ground started acquiring the name 'America' in the early 1820s for three reasons. First, there was a spirit of 'Americanism' among some of the squatters – they felt free of the town of Hastings in the same way that the Americans felt liberated from England after the Revolutionary War of 1775–83 and the War of 1812. Secondly, the Ground could only be approached from Hastings by going over some water (the Priory Stream, like crossing the Atlantic); and thirdly the name 'Priory' sounded similar to the American 'prairie'.

Although the boomtown was known occasionally as just 'America' in the 1820s and '30s, it does not seem to have been until the 1840s, after the clearance by the Crown, that it started being called 'the America Ground' – the Ground that had once been America.

There is no contemporary record of independence being declared by the 'Americans', and the only known occasion when the Stars and Stripes flag was flown was during the major town-wide celebrations of the passing of the 1832 Reform Act, which made parliamentary representation more democratic. On that day, a procession from the Ground carried a modified version of the Stars and Stripes during the celebrations – and then it was donated to the town hall by the not-so-independent 'Americans'.

The occupants of the Ground were too dependent on the jobs, economy and culture of Hastings to become truly independent of the town, in the same way that today Wales is too reliant on England to break away from it. And by no means all of the Ground's people were rebellious. Over a third of the Ground was in the hands of prominent members of the local establishment, most notably the three Breeds brothers, whose priority was maintaining good profit-generating ties with the many residents and businesses of Hastings and the surrounding countryside.

There have been claims that the Ground was home to many drunks, criminals, smugglers and loose-living women, and that it was quite unsafe for any visitor to venture near it after dark. But if it was sometimes unattractive, there is no evidence that the Ground was any worse than Hastings Old Town, where there were many more pubs, plus there was serious overcrowding, no sanitation, little fresh water and smugglers frequently going about their 'business'. A contemporary journalist who lived in the Old Town said everyday life on the Ground was little different from that in the Old Town.

However, it was the skirmishes over who could occupy which pieces of the Ground that alerted Whitehall in 1826 to the fact that possibly some form of anarchy was taking place on what was probably the Crown's land.

In response, the government in 1827 began preparing a legal enquiry into the Ground by carrying out a survey. This was to be followed by another survey in early 1829, which recorded a great mix of houses, tenements, workshops, stables, coach houses, piggeries, forges, warehouses, slaughterhouses, laundries, carpentries, bakers, sail lofts, rope works, saw pits and builders' yards (but very few pubs). The 1831 national census recorded 1,074 people living in the Holy Trinity Parish, nearly all of whom would have been on the Ground.

THE INQUISITION

The 1827 survey was followed by an 'inquisition' – a public inquiry – in the George Inn in Battle in December 1827, where anyone claiming to own any of the Ground was invited to prove it. As no one could do so (or, perhaps, wanted to), the jury ruled in favour of the Crown, which in law owned all English and Welsh foreshore by default if no other party could prove otherwise. All parties at the inquiry then had a very enjoyable meal at the Inn, the owners of which are believed to have been the Breeds family, the most prominent occupants of the Ground.

In mid-1828 legal notices to quit were given to all the occupants of the Ground, but with seven-year leases before enforcement. So the freedom followers occupying the once semi-independent America Ground had become tenants of the British government.

The Crown was taking a lenient approach with the long notices because of the money and labour many of the 'illegal' occupiers had invested in creating their premises, and in those seven years it seems that little (if any) rent collecting actually took place. The Breeds family would have been happy with the situation, as they could carry on running their large-scale businesses while only paying a minimal rent as a form of security (perhaps this had been arranged over dinner at the George?).

By coincidence, also in 1828 construction began of the new upmarket town of St Leonards, a mile to the west of the Ground. Initially many of the building workers in St Leonards squatted on the Ground, but then in the early 1830s land became available on the east side of the new St Leonards where they could build their own houses. Quite a few Ground residents then dismantled their existing homes and transported them to the new Shepherd Street/Norman Road area, where they were rebuilt, and where many are still standing.

The deadline for clearing the Ground was Christmas 1835, and the Crown's Commission of Woods and Forests then took possession of it. For the following fourteen years it was an open unused space, a piece of derelict 'ground' that was remembered as often being called 'America' – hence the name the 'America Ground' that gradually came into use in the 1840s.

But one part of the Ground was not cleared. This was Mr Boykett Breeds Jnr's large yard, with warehouses, storage sheds, a lime kiln and caves, which took up all the west side of today's Claremont. Mr Breeds and his father Mark had created the yard and Claremont itself in 1822 by cutting back the hill that sloped down from Prospect Place, forming the vertical cliff beside The Alley, on top of which the old *Observer* building stands. His yard covered all the level ground between the rock face and Claremont, where the Library and other buildings are today.

The Crown initially believed that they owned the piece of this Breeds's land that was nearer Claremont, because it was on shingle, but their cut-back hill to the west was not. In the end, Messrs Breeds were allowed to stay where they were.

In 1830 Boykett Breeds Jnr went bankrupt and had to sell most of his extensive property interests. These included his Bohemia House and large estate on the east side of Bohemia Road (including the site of today's Hastings Museum and Art Gallery), which were bought by the wealthy slave-owning Brisco family. Their history is in Appendix 7. From the 1870s the Breeds family focused their business activity on a large brewery they had in the Old Town.

The only surviving relic of the pre-1836 America Ground that is still in situ and visible today is the Breeds cliff face in The Alley, with one or more of the Breeds' caves in that cliff, but it is not known which. All the Ground's buildings had been demolished by 1836, although some were rebuilt in White Rock and central St Leonards. The known survivors of the 1830s 'house removals' that can still be seen today are listed in Appendix 2.

Crown Land

As the town expanded steadily in the 1830s, the Crown decided they had to protect their increasingly valuable potential building site from the sea. So in 1836–37 they built a large defensive sea wall from what is now Harold Place to the end of Robertson Street. This can still be seen inside the underground car park, forming all of the inland wall, a rare surviving example of how sea defences were built almost two centuries ago.

Not much happened on the America Ground – officially called the Crown Land – until 1849, when a wealthy Scottish businessman, Patrick Robertson, took a ninety-nine-year lease on most of it. Earlier he had become affluent from a controversial form of drug trading in the Far East, selling opium to the people of China, which enabled him to semi-retire to Hastings in 1847. Locally he became known as a gentlemanly benefactor of the poor, and he was elected as a liberal-oriented Conservative MP for Hastings from 1852. His life story is in Appendix 6.

In the early 1840s, the land north of the *c*.1580 embankment – where the Priory Meadow shopping centre is today – was still soggy undeveloped marshland, awaiting proper drainage.

However, by 1849 Robertson had seen the potential of creating what was to become known as the Regent Street of Hastings – Robertson Street – because of the imminent arrival of the railway in Hastings. The first railway line, from London via Lewes, had reached Bulverhythe in 1846, and in 1849 work was well under way on cutting the tunnels through hilly St Leonards to the station that was about to be built near the America Ground.

Robertson believed the trains would boost the town's economy, and therefore high-quality housing and shops near the station would be both popular and profitable. By 1850 the overspill from the cutting of the railway tunnels had been spread over the marshland, making it fit for development as the new town centre, and reinforcing his vision of the future.

Robertson employed the Crown Commission's architects Reeks & Humbert to design and oversee the layout and construction of the Ground. He obtained from the Crown two statues on plinths – one a lion, the other a unicorn – that had been made for the major redesign of Buckingham Palace then taking place. He placed them at either end of Robertson Terrace, where they still are today.

By the end of the 1850s most of the buildings now standing on the America Ground had been built. In later years the most significant changes were to be the erection of the Queens Hotel in 1863, the rebuilding in 1927 of the east end of Robertson Street as the Plummer Roddis department store (later Debenhams), the widening of the seafront with a car park underneath it in 1931, and bomb damage in the Second World War.

1

THE SHINGLE GROUND

The America Ground is based on shingle, which covers the entrance to what was a deep tidal estuary at the end of the Iron Age two millennia ago.

At that time Britain had between 1.5 million and 2.5 million people, living as farmers or small tribal groups, but with safeguarded areas (known as 'Iron Age forts') where they could meet for cultural, religious and security purposes. The East Hill (and possibly the West Hill)) was one such place, covering 60 acres in what is today part of Hastings Country Park. When the Romans invaded England they may have experienced little conflict in Kent and Sussex, as indigenous traders had had a working cross-Channel relationship with them for many years. It appears that the Romans allowed the existing way of life to

Hastings as it may have been soon after 1066. The town of Hastings is on top of White Rock, on the left, and the Priory Valley is a natural harbour, overlooked by the Castle.

continue where possible, in a period that saw the reorganisation and expansion of settlement across Sussex.

In Roman times there was no actual town of Hastings. The Priory Valley was a natural harbour formed by several watercourses running into the sea, mainly as the Priory Stream, between the West Hill and White Rock, which were then promontories extending much further into the sea than today. White Rock provided shelter from the predominant south-westerly winds, so trading vessels could moor safely alongside its east-facing slopes, where Claremont is today.

The Priory Valley in Roman and Anglo-Saxon times was one of only a handful of English harbours available for cross-Channel traffic, and this was probably the main reason why the town of Hastings was created in the ninth century, as a new national economy began to emerge based on increased trading and transport. The town itself was on top of White Rock, mostly on the section that has now been lost to the sea. No archaeological remains of the original Hastings have been found, although it is clear that an early medieval church called St Michael's stood just to seaward of where St Michael's Place is today.

The Priory Valley remained the port for Hastings through the Norman invasion of 1066 until around 1200, when the harbour entrance began silting up. From this time onwards Hastings would suffer from both constant coastal erosion, which ate into the cliffs, and from the long-shore west-to-east move-ment of shingle (the 'long-shore drift') that steadily blocked up the Priory Valley harbour.

During the thirteenth century the town of Hastings moved from White Rock into the Bourne Valley, but severe storms later that century forced the 'new town' of Hastings to move further up the Bourne Valley, to create what is now called the Old Town – even though it is the youngest 'town' of Hastings.

The Priory Valley was named after the Holy Trinity Priory, a small monastery that was set up around c.1189–99 by Walter de Scotney for the Augustinians (the Black Canons). Their lives involved preaching, administering the sacra-ments, tending the sick and giving hospitality to pilgrims and travellers.

The Priory itself was located where the southern end of Cambridge Gardens and the ESK Warehouse are today, at a much lower level than the existing buildings. Along the west side of the valley the Priory owned many acres of farmland, which formed the parish of Holy Trinity. The Priory had been dedi-cated to the Holy Trinity: the Father (God), the Son (Jesus) and the Holy Spirit (the power of God at work on Earth). The word 'trinity' comes from the word 'tri' meaning 'three' and 'unity' meaning 'one' – the three as one.

Part of the late twelfth-century Priory, on display in Hastings Museum and Art Gallery.

But the Priory had been built close to sea level, and although by the end of the fourteenth century the valley had partly filled with shingle, there were still strong surges of the sea into the Valley. These were so damaging that in 1417 the Canons abandoned the buildings and moved the Priory inland to Warbleton, near Rushlake Green in East Sussex.

The name of the Priory lives on in several placenames, especially Priory Road, one of the oldest roads in the town. For travellers coming into town from the Ridge, it provided access to the Priory via the West Hill when the sea was blocking the track along the beach below the Castle.

The Priory's new land at Warbleton had been donated by Sir John Pelham. The Pelhams were wealthy landowners in Sussex over many centuries, and they were to play a significant role in the history of the America Ground. As will be described later, Henry Thomas Pelham (1804–86), the third Earl of Chichester, son of Thomas (1756–1826), the second Earl, was to be involved in the Crown's key inquiry into the ownership of the America Ground in the late 1820s that resulted in it being cleared by 1835, when the government took possession of it.

By the fifteenth century the Priory Valley was unusable as a harbour, and from then through to the late nineteenth century there were repeated attempts to build a harbour arm-cum-breakwater in the sea on the west side of the Bourne Valley, roughly just to the west of today's harbour arm. The aim was to provide some shelter from the prevailing south-westerly wind for the fishing boats and trading vessels that worked off the beach in front of the town. But these harbours suffered repeated damage from the sea, so they needed constant repair, as was seen as recently as 2017–18 when today's harbour arm, built 1896–98, had to have major work carried out on it.

Some stones of the Priory survived in parts of buildings of the Priory Farm, seen here in the early nineteenth century.

In 1578 a petition was sent from the townspeople to Queen Elizabeth, saying that 'of late time the … harborough was at a sudden, by the great violence and extreme rage of the sea, broken downe and caried awaie. Sithence which time the Towne is much decayed.' Abandoning the idea of a harbour arm, the prominent Hastingers sought Her Majesty's backing for making the Priory Valley useable by vessels again. Their proposal was to turn the valley into a 'very good hauen [haven] … for the arriuing and sauegard of shippes, barkes, crayers and boates, to the great reliefe of the inhabitants and all merchants and travellers sayling along the narrowe seas [the English Channel].'[1] Its estimated cost was £4,000, about £1.84 million in today's money.

A 'haven' is a closed-in dock, like a marina, rather than a harbour arm projecting into the open sea. Queen Elizabeth gave her blessing, authorising the local establishment to start collecting funding for the scheme, and so work began. Within a year £2,000 had been spent, but then the money that the local businessmen had obtained went missing and construction had to stop. Historian William Camden wrote in 1586 that 'the contribution was quickly converted into private purses, and the publicke good neglected'.[2]

It seems that in about 1580 a sea wall of soil, and possibly rock, had been built across the Valley near the sea, roughly where Cambridge Road is today.

This may have been put on top of an already-existing trackway across the valley, which is likely to have been formed by people travelling along the coast once the Priory Valley had partly filled with shingle and silt. This trackway was probably on a 60ft-long embankment that had been laid in 1439 below the Priory, probably to help access across the valley. This suggests that by the early fifteenth century the valley had partly silted up.[3]

Prior to that, when the valley had been a natural harbour, travellers would have had to go inland along both sides of the valley to a point where they could cross the Priory Stream, probably in today's Alexandra Park. Stonefield Road may have been the main trackway along the east side of the valley in those years.

Parallel to the c.1580 sea wall across the valley, there appears to have been another wall further inland, where South Terrace is now. These two walls and the hillsides to the east and west of them would have formed the deep-water haven, where the Priory Meadow shopping centre is today.

There are no written records of the c.1580 haven, but several maps show that it existed. The first record is in the 1595 map by John Norden, showing 'The intended haven of Hastings'.

A century and a half later, two plans show that around 1750 the haven was still a clear geographical feature. Both plans were by local surveyor Samuel Cant, with that of 1746 (on page 28) being part of his survey of the borough boundaries. The 1750 plan is part of his depiction of the estate of local land-owner John Collier.

John Norden's 1595 map, with the 'intended haven' between White Rock and the Castle.

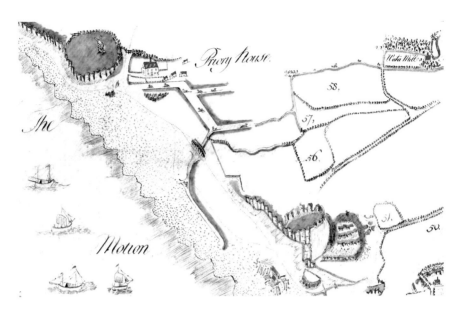

John Collier's 1750 plan, showing the remains of the c.1580 haven. White Rock, top left, has a windmill on it. The bridge is where today the streets come together in the town centre.

The two plans also show that there was a channel running out of the lake in the direction of White Rock through where Priory Street meets Cambridge Road today. At its south end, this channel had some form of sluice gate for regulating the flow of water into, and out of, the haven. The remains of it were discovered in the late eighteenth century, with the town's first-ever guide book ,in 1794, recording that a few years before, 'the remains of a sluice, deep gates and immense large timbers' had been found deep in the ground, indicating they had been there a long time.[4] They were described as being at the bottom of the 'Black Pond' in front of the Priory farmhouse (which stood in Cambridge Gardens, at its junction with Cambridge Road). Today, the sluice's location would be roughly the south end of Priory Street, and it may still be there, deep underground.

By the mid-eighteenth century, however, this channel had become unusable, and there was a drainage outlet at the southern corner of the lake. This was the Priory Stream resuming its natural course to the sea, where Harold Place is today. The failure to complete the haven in the 1580s would have meant that some form of a bridge had to be built across the stream, at the north end of Harold Place, so that the coastal traffic could continue.

The 1580s trickery by the leading Hastings businessmen that halted the haven scheme was probably the key factor in the setting up by the Crown in 1588 of a commission of inquiry into the mismanagement of the town of

Hastings. To regularise the controversial situation, a 'charter of incorporation' (usually referred to as the 'Elizabethan Charter') was passed in February 1589. The elusive, self-perpetuating cartel that had been running the town for many years was replaced by a new governing body, described as the 'Mayor, Jurats and Commonalty of the town and port of Hastings'. This was essentially the old self-interested ruling group by another name.

But from 1589 this was a new legally defined corporate body – Hastings Corporation – which had specific rights and responsibilities. These included ownership of the 'Stonebeach', the shingle that had been thrown up by the sea. This was to become a major source of both income and of legal conflict, from the late eighteenth century through to today, because of the great accumulation of such shingle in front of the town in the last two centuries. This beach has solidified and become building land – including the America Ground – and most of the borough's seafront has been constructed upon it.

The 1589 symbolic regularising of the town's corrupt mismanagement probably helped to raise national backing for the construction of a bigger new harbour arm in front of the Old Town. It was built in the summer of 1597, restoring the existing ruins of the earlier harbour. But on 1 November 1597, there 'appeared the mighty force of God, who with the finger of his hand at one great and exceeding high spring tyde, with a south-west wynd overthrow this huge worke in less than an hower, to the great terror and abasement of all beholders, … and to the manifest undoing of the town, which by reason thereof was left greatly indetted.'[5]

The ruins of the 1597 harbour, opposite where the west end of West Street is today.

During many decades after the 1597 disaster the remains of the harbour arm were partly patched up to try to provide at least some shelter. But a storm in late 1656 seems to have washed away all that remained of it.[6]

However, at the same time there were also attempts to raise enough money to complete the partially built *c.*1580 haven in the Priory Valley. In 1636 the Corporation sent a petition to King Charles I asking for financial aid to finish building it. The idea was agreed, and several promises of significant help were given, including £2,000 (about £425,000 today) from Sir John Baker (*c.* 1608–54), then the owner of the Priory land that included the haven. However, despite this major backing for the scheme, it seems that nothing came of it.

There is no record of how much of the haven existed then, but Sir John may have made some investments after 1636 to improve the quality of his farmland and to help him access customers in Hastings. Sir John's great-grandfather, also Sir John Baker (*c.*1489–1558), had been granted all the Priory land by Henry VIII in 1536 when it was dissolved during the Reformation. He was then the king's Attorney General and owner of Sissinghurst Castle in Kent.

The sea wall that had been built *c.*1580 roughly where Cambridge Road is today played a major role in shaping the future of the Priory Valley. The wall usually kept the sea out of the Valley, allowing the inland area first to become a mixture of badly drained marsh on the Valley bottom and farmland on its slopes until today's town centre buildings could be built in the nineteenth century. The sea wall's bridge over the Priory Stream was to become the focus

Looking from White Rock to the Castle in about 1750, showing what the Priory Valley was like before any development took place. In the foreground is the Priory Stream, with the bridge for the westbound road.

of that development, with the Albert Memorial clock tower being built on its site in 1863, while the road on the wall became the main route from Hastings west along the coast, and was also a way of heading towards London via White Rock and Silverhill.

The seaward side of the wall had become a resting place for the shingle coming along the coast on the long-shore drift, and by the late eighteenth century enough beach had built up there for it to start becoming a potential building site – and the America Ground.

The Priory Farm in 1784, before any other development in the Priory Valley.

2

PRE-1820: THE EARLY YEARS

It was the development of Hastings as a seaside resort and shipbuilding town in the late eighteenth century that gave birth to the America Ground.

Hastings was just a small fishing and trading port until the mid-eighteenth century, but then it slowly started to become a seaside watering place, after some medical 'experts' nationally promoted the unproven health merits of sea water. The boffins declared that there were medicinal qualities in a combination of ozone and sea water, taken internally and externally, for many complaints. Some physicians claimed that the sea was a natural saline bath of unlimited potential.

The new tourist role for the town was helped by the building of the Hastings–Flimwell turnpike road in 1753, which significantly improved the overland route to and from London, where the well-off bathers were usually coming from. Until then the badly maintained roads going north through the Weald were notorious for being unreliable, muddy, dangerous and almost unusable in winter.

Brighton sparked off a rapid rise in the popularity of the seaside for holidaymakers when the Prince of Wales visited that town in 1783 and effectively made it 'London-by-the-Sea', as it became known. The Industrial Revolution was rapidly increasing the wealth of the nation's upper class, who could spend their excess money on self-indulgence, and in the 1780s Hastings starting becoming one of their destinations. The *Gentleman's Magazine* in the summer of 1786 said: 'This town, from its pleasing situation near the sea, its bathing machines, the many pleasant walks and rides about it, diversified with the most agreeable prospects [views], is become, in proper season, the resort of a numerous and genteel company.'

The magazine reported that the only building in the Priory Valley, apart from the Priory Farm, was a lime kiln at the bottom of today's Wellington Square,

The Wellington Square lime kiln.

where the Poundstretcher store is today. The kiln, probably built in the early 1780s, was 'where great quantities of chalk are burnt into lime' to make mortar, which was essential in constructing new buildings. The chalk was brought by sea from the bottom of the cliffs just to the west of Eastbourne, and landed on the Hastings beach in front of the kiln, where the Carlisle pub is now.

By the late 1790s, lodging houses, libraries and other visitor facilities were being built in and around the Old Town, starting what was to be a steady growth of the town's economy into the nineteenth century. Much of the new development took place in front of the Old Town, on the shingle that had been accumulating there, and along to the west end of George Street (then called the Suburb).

Initially the Old Town had expanded as far as it could up the slopes of the East and West Hills, and into the gardens of the existing Old Town properties. However, the tops of the two hills, plus much of the upper Bourne Valley, were owned by the borough's most powerful local individual, Edward Milward Snr (1723–1811), who refused to build on most of this attractive land. But Milward, who was mayor of Hastings twenty-six times, was happy to see the town go west into the Priory Valley, not least because he had become owner of about a quarter of the Priory Farm's land, which he could sell at a good price to property speculators.[7]

A shipbuilding yard was one of the first developments to take place in the still-rural Priory Valley. The 1790s growth of the town had generated more demand for fishing boats and trading vessels, plus the government had an urgent need for armed cutters (single-masted sailing craft) to try to halt the steady increase in smuggling on the south-east coast. This prompted two young shipbuilders – William Ransom and William Ridley – to start a joint business, building a wide variety of vessels. The Ransom and Ridley yard, as it was known, was set up in the late 1790s on the beach where Wellington Place is today.

At about the same time some other buildings appeared in that immediate area, between the Castle and the Priory Stream (the stream is now under Harold Place). The other buildings were the large 1780s lime kiln, plus some stores and sheds, and possibly some small wooden houses.

There is no official record of how these buildings came to be there, as most, apart from the lime kiln, had been built on the beach, the ownership of which was unclear. The 1589 Charter that had set up Hastings Corporation said only that it owned the 'Stonebeach', without defining what or where that was. Could it only be the beach in front of the Old Town? Or could the Corporation own all of the beach within the 'Liberty' of Hastings, between Ecclesbourne Glen in the east and Glyne Gap in the west?

In 1746 Hastings Corporation published a map showing 'the Home Liberty, or Boundaries of the Town and Port of Hastings' as may have been understood in the 1589 Charter. On the plan, the boundaries along the coast were Glyne Gap and the glen, while inland the boundary line weaved through various points a mile or so from the sea.

But nationally a 'liberty' was usually defined as a district over which an authority only had certain privileges, which did not necessarily include actual ownership of the land. Plus, in the Priory Valley the coastal boundary on the map was on

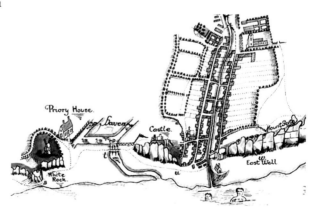

Hastings in 1746, showing the c.1580 haven. The town's boundary is the dotted line running past points S, T, U and W.

the inland side of what was to become the America Ground, thereby possibly excluding it. So Hastings Corporation may have had some rights over the 3 miles of beach within the Liberty, but it was uncertain what exactly that power was, and whether there was any control at all over what was to become the America Ground, lying outside the Liberty.

Until the town's development in the 1780s the geographic extent and definition of the Corporation's powers was not an important issue. However, the Corporation ensured it had full control over the beach in front of the Old Town by passing the 1789 Hastings Improvement Act, which gave the Corporation some powers to upgrade the town. But the Act only went as far west as the western boundary of the parish of St Clements, halfway along George Street (where Russell Court is), and did not include the beach in front of the Castle and the Priory Valley.

The 1789 Act created uncertainty over who owned, and therefore controlled, all of the beach between that Russell Court boundary and the Priory Stream. This indecision was fuelled by a feeling among most local people that all the beach along the coast was a form of 'common land' – land that ordinary people had a traditional right to use for everyday purposes. But the beach west of George Street was becoming hard ground, and therefore ready for development and profit-making by speculators as the town grew westward.

By the end of the 1790s the town's unplanned and erratic expansion over this new ground had reached the Priory Stream. This was to force the Corporation in 1820 to pass the second Hastings Improvement Act, which effectively

The west end of George Street in 1784. The building is the government-owned Gunners' House, built in 1759 to service the nearby battery of cannon.

gave some control over the beach between George Street and the Stream, but without stating that the Corporation actually owned it.

On the other side of the Stream were the unusable marshes north of the *c.* 1580 embankment, while south of it were several more acres of this beach-cum-land, ready for some type of development. But who owned it? In the early 1800s it was widely thought to be the Second Earl of Chichester. But if it was the Corporation, which seemed possible, why did they make no attempt to control it?

Eventually the beach area was to become known as the America Ground, but in the late eighteenth century it was usually called the Priory Land or the Priory Ground, as it was in the Priory Valley and next to the Priory Farm on the site of the old Priory. It was also known as the Shingles, the Outlands and the Waste Land. From here onwards in this story it will often just be called 'the Ground'.

People began occupying the Ground from the 1770s on a small scale, but the first significant development did not take place until 1800, when two ropewalks were built there. A ropewalk was a long straight narrow lane where lengthy strands of natural material (usually hemp) were laid side-by-side and then twisted together to make a long rope. There would be a twisting mechanism at one end of the walk and a fixing point at the other end. One end was mobile, moving towards the other end, because the twisting shortened the constituent parts of the rope. Many ropes on large sailing vessels had to be very

The old brig *Polymina*, next to the ropewalk.

long, and short pieces could not be joined together safely, so most ropes were made at great lengths and then cut down to size.

The developers in the autumn of 1800 were the three Breeds brothers, who laid out a ropewalk along the seaward edge of the Ground and erected a large brick building alongside it, plus several workshops. It is believed that they did this by paying a peppercorn rent to the then-apparent owner of the land, the Earl of Chichester.

It was the Breeds brothers who were to be the leading players in the whole history of the America Ground.

THE BREEDS BROTHERS

In the late eighteenth and early nineteenth centuries the Breeds family were the principal shipowners and merchants of Hastings. They were also bankers, property developers, farmers, shipbuilders, mail and coach proprietors, and brewers.

The brothers Thomas (1766–1839), James (1769–1845) and Mark (1774–1828) Breeds were the sons of Boykett Breeds Snr (1735–84), who had moved to Hastings from Rye in about 1760. He came from a seafaring family, and he set up what was to be the sole Hastings shipping business in the town until about 1801. This dominance of the town's main form of commercial transport made the Breeds family the leading merchants and traders until the improvement of the road network in the late 1830s.

Apart from shipping, the Breeds brothers were collectively and/or individually merchants and traders in coal, timber, iron, brewing, hops, grain and farming. Coal was especially important as it was the town's main form of heating and cooking. The Breeds owned and ran coaches, the other form of passenger transport to London and along the coast.

They had lime kilns, which were essential in the building trade as Hastings expanded rapidly, bringing it by sea in Breeds-owned vessels. In 1812 the brothers bought the Swan Inn on the High Street, the town's largest hotel, and from 1815 they played a leading role in the development of the Wellington Square area, thereby speeding up the rapid growth of the east side of the Priory Valley. In 1828 they built the beautiful terrace of Breeds Place, joining Pelham Crescent with Castle Street, now replaced by offices. All these enterprises together employed hundreds of people, many of whom were living on the Ground, or running their own businesses there.

Thomas Breeds, the oldest of the three sons, was the central figure in the family trio. In their early years they all worked together on many schemes, but later there were family disputes resulting in them tending to pursue separate interests. Mark, the most flamboyant of the brothers, died the earliest, in May 1828, and his son Boykett Jnr (1794–1861) was involved in the family business from an early age. In 1823 he and his uncle James bought the military's Halton barracks, later developed as the Halton housing estate, and in August 1824 they purchased the 90-acre Bohemia estate, including Bohemia House, built *c.*1818.

All this meant that for about fifty years, from around 1790 until the late 1830s, Boykett Breeds Snr's descendants were deeply involved in the growth of Hastings, and this was to include pioneering the development of the Ground.

The many sailing vessels used by the Breeds family were mainly going to London, for general supplies and passengers, and to northern England for coal. These large craft needed regular maintenance and repair, with a constant supply of sails, rope and rigging, and it was this servicing that prompted the Breeds to move onto a large space on the empty Ground in 1800.

As the Breeds were then a major part of the local establishment, their lease would probably have been informal and cheap, because the Ground was otherwise unused, and it was to the advantage of all local businesses to have a reliable

James Breeds's 124-ton collier brig *Telemachus*, built 1807, under repair on the beach.

form of transport to and from London, which the Breeds could supply them with from their new workplace.

At about the same time, in 1800–01, shipbuilder Thomas Thwaites, whose shipbuilding yard Thwaites and Winter was on the beach opposite the Castle, laid out another ropewalk, close to the inland side of that of the Breeds's, and built a house and rope workshop there. The 1804 *Hastings Guide* said the ropewalks were 'from 120 to 150 fathoms in length' (240 to 300yd), along most or all of the seaward side of the Ground.[8]

Around 1801 a Mr William Hamilton of Tenby in Pembrokeshire took possession of a large area of the Ground just inland from the Breeds's ropewalk and set up a shipyard. The Breeds quickly formed a partnership with Hamilton, turning a large part of the east end of the Ground into a busy shipbuilding and repair centre. Several vessels were soon built there, including two for the Admiralty: the 22-gun sloop *Rose*, and the 14-gun brig *The Racehorse*. The partnership did not last long, however, and the shipyard, with 'a mould-loft, six saw-pits, sheds, carpenters' shops and every other requisite', was advertised as being to let in early 1806.[9] The shipyard was rented out to other people until 1824, when two of the Breeds brothers, James and Thomas, took possession and divided it among themselves.

In 1806 the famous Scottish civil engineer John Rennie (1761–1821), who designed many bridges, canals and docks, produced a plan for a harbour in front of the Priory Valley, but nothing came of it.

In the first two decades of the nineteenth century several boats were converted into homes or workshops on the Ground. Some were old vessels that had come to the end of their seagoing lives, with the smaller ones being turned upside down.

Eliza Cook, publisher of a journal, recalled in 1851 how she had spent the summer of 1811 in Hastings. She described how:

impromptu houses, made of old boats covered in, the door unapproachable but by a ladder, gave life to [the Ground], assisted by the cackling of the geese and the braying of the donkeys belonging to the proprietors of these extraordinary edifices. I well remember entering into one of them in search of eggs, and where they were found was an old man, a child, a cat, and two kittens, three hens, and a duck, all in bed together most amicably; but the moment the woman approached to seek what I wanted, the old man began to grumble, the child to cry, the cats to mew, the duck to quack, and the laying hens to scream, till I became almost deaf and deranged by the various noises.[10]

Also on the Ground there were smugglers' boats, or half-boats, that had been seized by the Excise officers. These captured craft were stored in a special 'condemned yard', a fenced-in compound also known as the 'Black Hole', opposite the west entrance to Pelham Crescent. The craft were sold by public sale, either whole or cut in half. After the decline in smuggling during the 1830s, the yard was leased in 1840 to nearby lodging house owners, who wanted a more attractive view from their windows, and who turned it into a garden. A new condemned yard was opened in Rock-a-Nore Road, which closed in 1852 and the Fishermen's Church (now the Fishermen's Museum) was built on its site.

In 1807 James Breeds hauled an old brig (i.e. a two-masted square-rigger), the *Polymina*, up on top of the beach next to the ropewalks and turned it into two tenements (picture page 30). It was such a desirable residence that the first two tenants, Thomas Page and John Prior, were still there in 1829! The *Polymina* was the second recorded living place installed on the Ground, the first being a house built for a Mrs Brazier before 1807.

Another large old brig, the *Noah's Ark*, was also installed on the Ground. When large numbers of squatters began moving onto the Ground around 1820 it seems that most of the boats were removed, and in the Crown's 1829 survey of the Ground only the *Polymina* and the remains of a much smaller vessel were recorded.

Noah's Ark.

The Breeds family also played social roles in the town. From 1817 James let the loft over his warehouse at the west end of the ropewalk be used as a school by the Saunders charity. The charity had been without a school and schoolmaster for several years because of mismanagement of its funds by some of the local establishment.

NEW TOWN 1800–20

While Hastings was growing rapidly in the first two decades of the nineteenth century, other development took place on the Priory Ground, alongside the Breeds. A new and bigger wooden bridge able to take carriages and large wagons was built over the Priory Stream in 1800–01, thereby both making the Ground more accessible for new neighbours of the Breeds, and improving the western coast road.

England's long-running war with France temporarily halted in March 1802 but resumed in May 1803, prompting major military activity and investment in the Hastings area. Fearing French invasion, Hastings became a garrison town, with the War Department in 1804 building a large military base on several acres of land at Halton (above the Old Town), and another barracks at Bopeep in west St Leonards. Also in 1804 the Department began making the 28-mile-long Royal Military Canal across Romney Marsh, and in 1805 work started on building seventy-four Martello Towers along the south coast. For all this major military construction work, the Department had to buy large amounts of raw materials from local businesses, and many hundreds of builders and labourers had to be employed. At the same time the Hastings shipyards supplied the Navy with vessels and equipment, and privateers were built for Hastings boat-owners and crews who wanted to capture French trading craft.

This major boosting of the town's economy made many local businessmen wealthy, leading some of them to invest in new schemes. By as early as 1803 the Breeds family, plus three other speculators, had generated enough spare cash to be able to start the Hastings Bank, only the second bank set up in Hastings.

As the fears of a French invasion faded away in following years, and Hastings attracted more visitors, landowners started building new properties – especially lodging houses in the Old Town and along under the Castle cliff. In 1811 work began on York Buildings, but it was the boom tourist year of 1814 and the end of the French war in 1815 that brought the major development on the east side of Priory Valley, starting with Wellington Square, the York Hotel and Russell Street.

The success of the Battle of Waterloo on 18 June 1815 may have prompted what the *Sussex Weekly Advertiser* called on 28 July a 'whimsical game of cricket' on what was known as the Rock Fair's Ground, where Claremont is today. It was played by:

> 22 aged, lame and infirm men belonging to Hastings, who took their departure together for the field of action, from before the Swan Inn [on the High Street], amid the huzzas of the surrounding multitude, in a wagon arched over with green boughs, and drawn by four oxen, ornamented with ribbons, one of the party officiating as charioteer, with white reins fastened to the horns of the animals … preceded by a car of minor description (a donkey vehicle) and two Egyptian ponies, which exhibited four musicians, with their faces *elegantly* be-smeared with common rouge, contrasted and variegated with *soot*, to the no small diversion of a great number of spectators.[11]

The Rock Fair was the town's oldest annual social gathering, held every 26–27 July on the west side of the Ground on a slightly raised piece of land called Rock Fair Green; the full story of the town's fairs is in Appendix 5.

The Rock Fair in July 1811. Today's Cambridge Road is on the left; Robertson Street is on the right, with America Ground buildings beyond it. The smoke is from the lime kiln. The two masts are a brig at Ransom and Ridley's shipyard.

Meanwhile, on the rest of the west side of the Valley, the Priory Farm remained as just farmland, but the Ground became the home for many businesses and people that could find no space elsewhere in Hastings. In 1819, there were eleven 'neat cottages, very airy, with a near sea view' providing lodgings along the ropewalk and nearby, according to *Powell's Guide to the Lodging Houses of Hastings.*

After 1815 many local fishermen who had been in the Navy were demobbed, and, finding it hard to make a living, took up smuggling on a large scale. In response, the government in 1817 set up the armed Coast Blockade Service (CBS) – the Navy on shore – with a station on the Ground, possibly built in 1819. The CBS (later called the Coastguard) was a police force before the police had been set up.

However, the weather was a significant danger for all users of the Ground, for there was a constant risk of gales combining with high tides to break over the low-lying beach. The sea would also sometimes surge up the channel of the Priory Stream, and through the beach under the Ground to flood the former haven, then known as the Priory Brooks. This happened on 18 November 1808, giving the Brooks the appearance of a lake, and was repeated on 8 November 1810, flooding Bulverhythe as well. In October 1812 very high tides swept inland once again.

The worst combination of high tide and strong wind for many years occurred in October 1820, causing much damage to the buildings on the Ground.[12] It also swept away the twenty-year-old wooden bridge over the Priory Stream, which was replaced in 1821 by a bigger and better bridge made of brick and stone, with three lamps on each parapet. This was to help the development of all of the west side of the valley in the following years. (More details in Chapter 3.) In 1819 the part of the road going round the seaward side of White Rock (another part of the road going west along the coast) was widened and improved following storm damage.

The 1821 national ten-year census showed how much the Ground had developed in the first two decades of the nineteenth century. The Ground lay within the parish of Holy Trinity, which was essentially the land of the Priory Farm, plus the Ground. In the 1801 census there were just ten residents in the parish, probably all living on the farm. In 1811 there were seventy-six people in the parish, and in 1821 there were 294 residents. As there had been little if any development on the farmland in 1801–21, these figures show how many people had moved onto the Priory Ground in just twenty years.

A Coast Blockade officer –
and a smuggler?

In the next twenty years the number of residents rocketed to 1,074 in 1831, but then plummeted to just nine in 1841. These figures reflect the dramatically rapid 'take-over' of the Ground from 1822, and the clearance of the Ground by the Crown in 1835. From 1822 the Ground effectively started becoming the 'America' Ground in spirit, if not in name, as hundreds of people squatted the land whose ownership was uncertain and which seemed to lie beyond the control of any local authority.

3

THE 1820s:
BOOM TOWN

In the early 1820s the piece of land that was to become the America Ground was flooded – not by the sea, but by people. They were the urgently needed new workforce who came into Hastings to help the town's rapid development.

Construction of the Wellington Square and Russell Street area had begun in 1816, and it was to carry on through the 1820s. Meanwhile, on the seafront, the owner of Hastings Castle – Thomas Pelham, the 2nd Earl of Chichester (1756–1826) – decided to have a large part of the cliff below the Castle removed, so that he could build there. In 1820 he constructed the big eight-house terrace of Pelham Place (where the Deluxe Leisure Centre is today), and then in 1823 he started on Pelham Crescent, with its underlying arcade and shops, plus St-Mary-in-the-Castle Church, which were all completed by early

Marine Parade in the early 1820s. The tall buildings are Pelham Place, built in 1820, the forerunner of Pelham Crescent and the development of the western seafront.

1828. The architect was Joseph Kay (1775–1847). The architectural ensemble was then completed by the Breeds Place terrace of eight houses joining the west end of the Crescent, designed to balance Pelham Place.

These new upmarket residences, lodging houses and entertainment venues attracted many well-off people to the town. They could stroll along the Marine Parade below the Castle, read newspapers in the libraries overlooking the sea, imbibe in one of the hotels, take a dip in the briny or in the seafront bath-house, watch the many fishermen and shipbuilders at work, or go for a stroll along the beautiful cliffs and glens to the east.

All the large-scale building work taking place in Hastings generated a press-ing need for builders' yards, workshops, stables, carriage sheds and homes for many of the labourers and craftsmen who could construct these premises. As there was no cheap or useable undeveloped land in the town where these prem-ises could be built in the early 1820s, the out-of-town Ground was an obvious place to go.

Not only was it close to the many building sites, but Hastings Corporation did not seem to be trying to control what took place there. It was possible that the 1589 charter may have given the Corporation some authority over the Ground, but the Commissioners were keeping the problem at arm's length, temporarily at least, because the Ground was accommodating a much-needed workforce that could not be housed elsewhere.[13] The marshland on the inland side of the c.1580 embankment remained too wet to use.

By 1820 it had become known that the Corporation did not seem to be trying to stop people squatting on the Ground, and as a result many began moving in, finding their own spare piece of rent-free land. This was actually a bonus for the developers carrying out the building work around the town, because the overheads of the squatters, whether home seekers or service provid-ers, would be lower than those of normal rent payers, so the squatters would be cheaper to hire, and the cost of the construction would be lower and the profit higher. So squatting was of mutual benefit to the squatters, the builders, the landowners, local businesses and Hastings Corporation (which itself was effectively run by business people and landowners).

Until about 1820 the occupants of some bigger pieces of the Ground – espe-cially the Breeds brothers – had come to some arrangement with the Earl of Chichester, who at that time seemed to be the Ground's landlord. The brothers would have been paying what was possibly only a peppercorn rent to ensure that their large-scale investment had some security.

But from roughly 1820 the Ground started becoming regarded as common land, free to anyone. Thomas Brett described how in 1822:

> a general rush was made by the townspeople to seize upon certain plots for building purposes. Stones, bricks, boulders, posts and other materials were used for setting out the boundaries thus acquired without so much as the asking; and many a skirmish … resulted as a consequence of one appropriator removing his neighbour's landmarks.[14]

It was the Corporation's reluctance to exercise any control over the land west of the Priory Stream that led to it becoming known initially as 'America', and then later as the 'America Ground'.

The name America became popular because the new area was independent of local authority control, like the USA was free from English rule, plus it was over the water (over the Priory Stream, rather than over the Atlantic) and it was often known as the 'Priory', which sounded like the American 'prairie'.

The full name 'America Ground' only seems to have come into widespread use in the late 1840s. From around 1820 it was also called No-Man's Land and Squatter-Land.

Brett said that 'Quarrels and fights over disputed boundaries on "Squatter-Land" at the Priory were of frequent occurrence.'[15]

He recalled:

> It was in 1822 when the rush to the Priory waste was made to seize, without purchase, that 'no man's land' from which resulted turbulent scenes of rivalry, to some of which I was an eye-witness. On the 29th of April [1822] two persons had nearly completed each a building on that ground, when a previous disputation of right rose to a fierceness that induced one of them, in a fit of exasperation, to pull down the other's wall. The latter retaliated upon his rival's structure, and so strenuously was the work of destruction pursued that in less than an hour considerable portions of both buildings were levelled with the ground. Fortunately, little, if any, personal injury was sustained, and both parties, with their helpers, set themselves afterwards to repairing the work thus destroyed.
>
> There were many similar disputes with persons who had marked out boundaries for themselves one day, to find that their landmarks had been removed on the next by other scramblers.[16]

The *Sussex Weekly Advertiser* reported that on 10 March 1823, 'An affray took place between two parties … respecting some buildings which they were erecting, as to the right of situation. The assailants were beaten off without any serious accident, and a blue flag hoisted denoting victory, by their opponents on the premises.'[17] Hostilities resumed on 26 June, but this time more violently, ending with wounds and bruises. That night, windows were broken in the homes of Mark and James Breeds, so they presumably were involved in the dispute.[18]

The reason why the blue flag was a symbol of victory in a struggle is not recorded, but it may have its origin in the blue flag that was the banner of the Republic of West Florida, a republic of English-speaking people in parts of Louisiana east of the Mississippi River who broke away from the Spanish West Florida in September 1810. However, the republic's independence only lasted three months, as it was then annexed by the United States. So the Ground's blue flag may have its origin in the new USA.

It is often stated that the American Stars and Stripes flag was flown on the Ground, showing that its occupiers were declaring independence from Hastings and/or England.

The American flag was a topical symbol of being free from authoritarian rule, and many Ground residents probably had political aspirations that drew on what had happened over the water in the USA. If Hastings Corporation on the other side of the Priory Stream was letting the squatters be 'independent', why not fly the flag of independence? So it is quite likely that the flag was flown for political reasons, but not to actually declare self-government, because most of the Ground's residents and businesses were probably dependent for their incomes from their employers, friends and relatives over the water in Hastings.

There is only one contemporary record of the Stars and Stripes actually being flown. This was during the large-scale public celebrations of the passing of the Reform Act in 1832, which brought about some of the parliamentary changes the flag-flyers had been seeking. The events will be described later, in Chapter 6.

Conflicts between rival squatters took place under the eyes of the CBS, which had a large Watch House on the edge of the beach at the centre of the ropewalk. The Priory Watch House was the headquarters of the Sussex Eastern Division of the CBS, overseeing the twenty-seven CBS stations between Camber and Eastbourne. There were nine officers and twenty-two servicemen based at the Priory station.

The Service was mainly aimed at stamping out smuggling, a widespread enterprise by much of the local population, which climaxed through the 1820s because of a great deal of poverty. Brett recalled: 'Not only was the Priory the battle-ground of the so-called squatters; it was also the scene of many a conflict between smugglers and Coastguards.'[19]

It is ironic that the smugglers and the Blockade men may have been sailing in vessels built at the same shipyard in Hastings. And the craft of captured smugglers could have been sawn in half at the condemned yard very close to the shipyard that built it! The Ransom and Ridley shipyard, where Wellington Place is now, built many anti-smuggling cutters for the government, including in 1825 an extra-large, over-150-ton vessel that could carry fourteen cannon.

LAYOUT

The layout of the Ground, as can be seen in the Crown's 1829 plan below, was shaped very much by the shipyard, ropewalk and other structures put in place by the Breeds brothers early in the 1800s.

The Breeds's ropewalk provided a baseline from which other spaces were laid out. The Priory Stream was the physical eastern border of any development

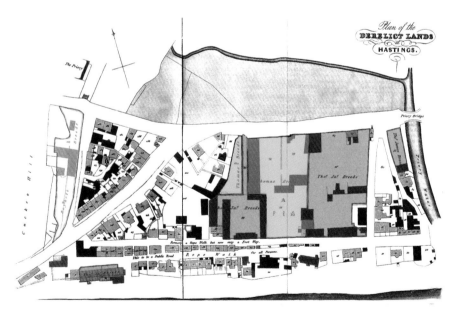

The 1829 plan shows the Ground occupied by the Breeds family. Red is James Breeds, green Thomas and yellow is Boykett Jnr, son of Mark. The large black building at the centre of the bottom line of buildings is the Watch House. The Breeds's ropewalk is the southern one. The grey area at the top is the unusable marshland. The plan has been coloured by this book's author; it is described in more detail in Chapter 4.

on the Ground, while the boundary on the north side was the road from the Priory Stream bridge, following roughly the path of today's Cambridge Road as far as Claremont, the western boundary.

For many centuries there had been some form of bridge here. Without a bridge, coastal travellers would have to go inland along the side of the Priory Valley to where Alexandra Park is today, then cross the narrower stream and come back down the other side of the Valley.

In late October 1820 the wooden bridge built in 1800–01 was washed away in a severe gale, which also damaged many buildings close to the sea.

Above, the wooden Priory Bridge over the Priory Stream in 1816. It was washed away in 1820 and replaced in 1821 by the brick and stone bridge, below, seen here in 1830. The large house in the distance is the Priory Farmhouse, with farm buildings on the right. The bending road is the predecessor of the straightened Cambridge Road, built in 1836–38.

In mid/late 1821 a bigger and better bridge made of brick and stone was built, costing £504 (about £60,000 today). This was to help both the travellers and occupants of the Ground.

The Hastings–Bexhill road ran to the west from the bridge on top of the c.1580 embankment, and then curved south-westwards. On the west side of the curve was a triangle of slightly raised ground, now the triangle of Claremont, Trinity Street and Robertson Street. This was the traditional site of the annual Rock Fair, the town's biggest social event, held every 26 and 27 July since time immemorial. It was a very popular get-together, attracting large crowds to eat and drink, play games, meet friends and watch many entertainments. It was traditionally believed that a cricket field had been created on some of the Ground in the eighteenth century by spreading soil on it, and that this helped pave the way for the development of the Ground.[20]

But in 1822 the Rock Fair's land was taken over by the Ground's new occupants, and the Fair moved to the top of White Rock. The full history of the Rock Fair is in Appendix 5.

The 1822 relocation of the Fair was the result of Mark Breeds and his son Boykett Jnr buying the part of White Rock (often then called Cuckoo Hill) east of Dorset Place, sloping down into the Priory Valley. They then cut back the slope to create a large workspace, forming Claremont at the same time, as shown on the plan on page 46. Until then there had been a steep slope from where Portland Place is today, down to where the buildings on the west side of Claremont now are. The Breeds cut this back to where the cliff is in what is now called The Alley, and they probably deposited the removed soil and rock where the triangle is today.

Mark and Boykett Jnr built a trade centre on this new land, with a coal warehouse, a wood-sawing house, a saw pit and several warehouses. The most prominent feature was a very tall lime kiln built in 1823 against the cliff. It was 'a brick pyramid of considerable elevation', said the *Sussex Weekly Advertiser*, 'which may be seen at great distances from the surrounding country, answering the purpose of a beacon or land mark', and could be inserted on mariners' charts.[21]

At the north end of their land the Breeds probably made a large cavern that today is part of the sub-basement of the old *Observer* building in Cambridge Road. The entrance to this warehouse was in The Alley, where the Breeds also probably made one or more of the small caves still to be seen in the rock face. In addition, the Breeds created the roadway of Claremont in order to provide access from their premises to both the Hastings–Bexhill road, and

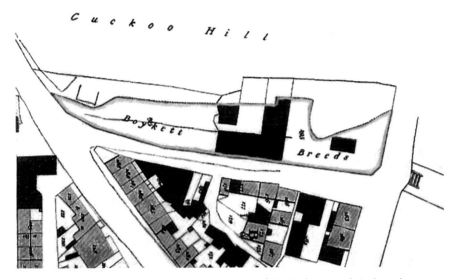

In the 1829 plan, the green-encircled area is the part of the Boykett Breeds Jnr's workspace abutting Claremont which the Crown believed it owned. The area marked off above that is the section of Cuckoo Hill which Breeds had cut back, creating the cliff-face.

to the beach beyond that road, where their seagoing vessels could load and unload their goods.

Claremont was initially called St Michaels Street, but was later named after the well-known Dowager Lady Clermont, 'a leader in the role of fashion',[22] who was a popular resident of Hastings until her death in late 1820. Three houses later built at the junction of Claremont and White Rock were named after her.

But the Breeds's Claremont centre became a problem for the Crown in 1827 when the government claimed ownership of the Ground. Most of the Ground was on shingle, which the Crown could maintain that it owned, whereas about a third of the Breeds's centre was not on beach but on the cut-back hillside, which was theirs legally. Much, if not all, of the centre escaped the 1835 clearance of the America Ground, and it continued in use for many years after that.

By the mid-1820s Mark Breeds had effectively retired, and his son Boykett Jnr had taken over the running of his side of the family businesses. In 1827 Boykett Jnr had a 150-ton brig (a two-masted square-rigger) built and named *Mark Breeds* after his father. It was built at the Thwaites and Winter shipyard, opposite the west end of Pelham Crescent, and was launched on 26 June.

Boykett Jnr at that time was based in the Claremont yard, and in the autumn of 1827 he advertised his many businesses as 'Coal merchant, grocer, dealer in

The view from the bottom of White Rock in the early 1820s, before the 1824 storms.

fir timber, deals, laths, lead, Roman cement, corn, malt, hops, London porter and stout, linseed, rape and mustard cake'. He had '450 tons of shipping employed in the Hastings trade'.[23]

The Ground seems to have been fully occupied by 1824, but in that year two severe storms caused much damage to many of the buildings, highlighting how vulnerable the area was to the sea. On 24 July 1824 a temperature of 80°F was followed by several hours of thunder, lightning, rain, flooding and hailstones said to be up to 3in in diameter.

On 24 November high tides driven by a gale destroyed many buildings on the Ground. James 'Tring' Brazier, a shoemaker with premises on the Ground, 'being a strong man, earned many shillings by carrying persons through the flood on either side of the Priory Bridge', recalled Thomas Brett. He described the passengers as 'man-back riders'.[24]

The Hastings–Bexhill road going round the bottom of White Rock also suffered regular damage by the sea, so in the winter of 1825–26 the road was improved and a wall was put up in front of it. This was to encourage the development of the White Rock seafront in the following years, especially when construction of the new town of St Leonards began in 1828.

4

THE
AMERICAN LIFE

The *Hastings Observer* in 1899 said that 'During the "squatter" period [the Ground] acquired the nickname of "America", and in spite of their boundary squabbles its inhabitants displayed considerable clannishness, so that the "Americans" and their Stars and Stripes banner figure rather conspicuously in the politics and festivities of the period.'25

But Thomas Brett, born in Hastings Old Town in 1816, recalled that:

Both in conversation and in print it used to be stated that the Priory people were 'a lawless and disreputable lot', but it could be easily shown that many hard things were laid to their charge which were not justified by facts, and that as a whole, the 'Americans' were quite as law-abiding and respectable as an equal number of their traducers. Even my old friend, the late Mr John Banks, in his *Smugglers and Smuggling* [a Hastings book published in 1873] tells his readers that 'It became a locality for the drunken and the lawless, and it was really not safe to pass over it after dark'.

Now, as I resided there several years with my parents, and knew almost every one of the inhabitants, it behoves me to say that the above quoted statement is a libel, begotten of prejudice. There were a few bad characters but even these were not worse than the same class in the Old Town from whom they had separated.

Brett as a youngster also occasionally worked for his uncle Thomas Ranger, who had a blacksmiths, a carpentry and a pub at what is now the junction of Claremont and Trinity Street. He continued:

It was even said that most of the inhabitants of the Priory Ground lived in a state of concubinage, as proved by the very few marriages that took place. This, too, either through malice or ignorance, was the reverse of the truth.

Brett believed that the people of the Priory Ground 'were as law-abiding as those of the Old Town, and that their observance of marriage rites and duties were no less regular'.[26] Parish records show that between 1822 and 1835 inclusive there were 180 weddings at the Church-in-the-Wood in Hollington when at least one of the couple lived in the Holy Trinity parish – and all the parish residences bar one (the Priory farmhouse) were on the Priory Ground.

So what was life like for the thousand or so residents and workers on the Priory-cum-America Ground in the 1820s?

There was no laid-on water supply or sanitation, but neither was there in Hastings Old Town, where the Bourne Stream was both a sewer and the only significant source of 'fresh' water. For cleaner water in the Old Town, you, or your children, had to fill your jugs a long way up the stream, or pay to use the spring in George Street (behind what is now the Pump House pub), or maybe have some luck with the spring coming out of the cliff in Rock-a-Nore Road, where the East Well is today.

In the Ground, the sewage could be deposited in the Priory Stream or the sea. Nearly fresh water came from the Stream further inland, but there were also three better sources of it.

Brett recalled that there was a recess in the rock behind what is now 24 or 25 White Rock 'from which flowed a copious spring, useful alike to man and beast. It was from this spring that a considerable number of the nicknamed "Americans" … obtained their drinkable water, it being conveyed to them in budges [leather buckets] and doled out at a halfpenny a pailful.'[27]

Hollington Church-in-the-Wood, where the 'Americans' married.

The Priory Farm and farmhouse in 1821. White Rock is in the background. Parts of the old Priory are said to have been used in one or more of the farm buildings.

The second source was a spring at what is now the north end of Cambridge Gardens and Priory Street, from which water, 'by being pumped into budgens, was supplied at a penny per load (two pailfuls) to the inhabitants of "squatter-land"'.[28]

Brett went on to say that the third source was a small stream in a Priory Farm field, where Cornwallis Gardens are today. Here, by the kindness of the farmer, 'certain inhabitants of the Priory had gratuitous access [to the water], together with the leaches that were frequently found in the dipping place'.

The Priory Farm – a farmhouse, barns, oasts and granaries – dominated the landscape immediately to the north of the Ground. The buildings were in today's Cambridge Gardens, with the white weather-boarded farmhouse standing on what is now the left-hand side of the Gardens, just as it turns in from Cambridge Road.

But the buildings were much lower than the roads are today, being nearly on a level with Claremont, which formed a junction with Cambridge Road. That road was made much higher when it became part of the turnpike road redevelopment of the late 1830s, which cut through the steep slope of the hill and spread the excavated soil and stone down towards the Priory Bridge. Until the late 1830s the only road going from the Bridge to the north-west was Dorset Place, curving round the top of White Rock and then going up to Bohemia Road. The turnpike connected the bottom of Cambridge Road and Bohemia Road, as we know Cambridge Road today.

The Priory Bridge was where all today's roads in the town centre come together, but the ground level was several feet lower than now. The western part of the town centre, Havelock Road, Station Road and the Priory Farm surroundings were built on top of the 1848–50 spoil from the railway tunnels.

On the north side of Cambridge Road was the site of the half-built sixteenth-century haven. The road itself was roughly on top of the haven's sea wall, and the ground inland of it – often called the Priory Brooks – was low and liable to flooding, this being a leftover from its partial excavation to form the haven. The west side of the haven was where Devonshire Road is today, with the east and north sides being Stonefield Road. The many acres of the Brooks were regularly flooded or saturated by the Priory Stream and the sea – sometimes together – and often froze over in winter to form a popular skating and sliding scene.

But despite this semi-rural landscape, it was not all peace and quiet in Hastings in the 1820s. The rapidly developing town had no police or fire service, and in February 1824 a special public meeting in the town hall on the High Street called for something to be done to prevent 'a repetition of nocturnal depredations, robberies, etc, and for the protection of property in cases of fire or other accidents'. On 1 March the town's Commissioners agreed to hire watchmen to patrol the town, and a month later it was reported that they had done good 'not only in preventing the commission of crimes but in suppressing riotous and disorderly conduct'.[29]

THE HOUSING ESTATE

By the mid-1820s, on the Ground there were over 200 dwellings, warehouses, workshops, huts (some with upturned hulls of fishing boats for roofs), pig pounds and a whitewashed Coast Blockade Station. All these buildings can be seen on the 1829 plan, on page 8, the frontispiece.

The variety of homes ranged from ramshackle wooden cottages to solid brick-built structures. Robert Moss's 1824 *History of Hastings* said the ropewalks 'are surrounded by cottages recently erected, all of them commanding near views of the sea, and which, though constructed in a variety of styles, are most of them neat airy buildings'.

The spring 1829 survey of the Ground for the 1830 Crown report (details in Chapter Five) found there were fifty-eight houses, forty-three cottages and

A house on the Ground, with a shrimper setting off down the beach.

forty-nine 'tenements' (flats or parts of houses). Each of these three catego-
ries had 'several' more, without saying how many, so there were more than
150 residences of some kind.

A landmark of the Ground was the large former sailing vessel *Polymina*, split
into two tenements. The 1830 report also said that on the Ground there was
an 'old boat, or part thereof' and a 'timber cottage on wheels, canvas roof' – a
caravan.

The details of who was living on the Ground are in Appendix 3.

The 1829 survey does not record the number of people living on the Ground,
but the ten-yearly census of 1831 reported that 1,074 people were living in the
Holy Trinity parish, where the only significant dwelling outside the Ground
was the Priory Farm. In the rest of Hastings (excluding St Leonards) there were
7,982 residents, so about 12 per cent of the 9,056 population of Hastings in
1831 were living on the Ground.

In 1821 there had been 294 people in the parish, with 5,670 in the rest of the town, making a total of 5,964. Only 2 per cent of the town were then living on the Ground.

In the parts of the Ground not occupied by the Breeds family there was considerable overcrowding, but it was a similar story in the Old Town, where many tiny houses were being built in the back gardens of numerous properties on the High Street and All Saints Street.

There were no local authority rules or regulations for the Ground's residents and landlords to stick to, as they were outside the Hastings borough boundary, so the housing could be of any shape, size or quality.

THE INDUSTRIAL ESTATE

The 1829 survey also catalogued the large number of non-residential buildings on the Ground. There were about fifty large buildings, plus many more that were smaller.

The Ground was 8.56 acres (3.46 hectares) in size, and about a third of this was in the hands of the Breeds, with James occupying the largest amount, about 20 per cent of the total area. He and brother Thomas had initially, in 1800, moved onto about 30 per cent of the Ground together, probably after leasing it from, or coming to an arrangement with, the Earl of Chichester. But some years later they split the area between themselves.

In the 1829 survey, James had a very large yard that contained a rope warehouse, a tar house, a cottage, a house, a coal yard, a shed, a block and mast workshop, eleven tenements, a coke oven, two eight-stall stables, a timber yard, a stonemason's workshop and yard, several piggeries and a sawpit. Plus he owned a large wheelwrights workshop and yard next to the Priory Stream.

James also had the Pelham Mews, the base of the town's main coach service and with many stables for the well-off visitors staying in places such as Pelham Crescent. This was a large yard with stables, stalls and coach houses on all sides, with rooms for the servants above many of the stalls. This was all run by Edward Stevens, who had his own house roughly where Trinity Street is today.

In addition, James also had a rope warehouse at the west end of the rope-walk, where 1 Carlisle Parade is now. This probably contained a machine for winding the rope on the ropewalk, while the loft had been used as a school by the Sander's Charity, although this not recorded in the survey. But the survey does mention a schoolroom near the warehouse, on the east side of Claremont, very close to its junction with today's Robertson Street. This was not owned by James Breeds, but by a Mr James Hayes. The property was described as 'School Room and Wheelers Shop (Timber)', probably meaning it was a wheel-making workshop, with a school above it. Brett said the school was run by a Mr Barnes, and some Wesleyan meetings were held there in 1829, with the Curate of St Mary's Church at the same time holding services in the school-room over the rope warehouse.[30]

Close to his rope warehouse James also had a small terrace of houses, while at the other end of the ropewalk he had what the survey called 'A small tene-ment, formerly an old boat, or part thereof. Occupier: Late Henry Tilden.'

James's best-known property was a large boat, a brig called the *Polymina*, pic-tured on page 30. It was described as 'An old hulk, now in two tenements. This old brig was brought here 22 years since [i.e. in 1807], and was then the first house on the property (except Mrs Brazier's house on the Mount), and both the present tenants lived in the brig when it was first brought.' The tenants were Thomas Page and John Prior.

Between James's Pelham Mews and his very large yard was an equal-sized yard occupied by his brother Thomas Breeds.

In Thomas's yard were two carpenters' workshops, a sail loft, two houses, a washhouse, a large shed, open sheds, a saw pit, stables, a coach-making work-shop, two plasterers' workshops, a forge and a big 'coach manufactory', making and maintaining the coaches that provided the Hastings–London coach ser-vices. Thomas also had a fairly large piece of open ground on the other side of the Pelham Mews, let to the Mews manager Edward Smith.

In the 1829 survey, Boykett Breeds Jnr (son of Mark, who had died in May 1828) had a large piece of the Ground, occupying all the land on the west side of Claremont. About a third of his space was where the hill had been cut back, and was not claimed by the Crown because it was not beach. On the map, area A (the north end) was a 'Sawing house/pit etc.' Area B was 'Stabling, ware-houses etc.' Area C (the south end) was 'Coal warehouse, kiln, yard etc.' There is no record of Boykett having any tenants.

Over the road from Boykett Jnr was one of the very few pubs in the Ground. If the Blacksmith's Arms was still standing, it would be roughly on the north corner of Trinity Street and Claremont. It is not recorded in the early 1829 survey, having apparently been converted later that year from the cabinet-making workshops of Mr William Honiss. The conversion was carried out

Going paddling in the early 1820s; on the left is the Coast Blockade Service Watch House.
In 1824 (below) the ropewalk can be seen bottom right, and Wellington Square is being built
under the Castle.

by builder Edward Towner, who was after that engaged in the construction
of many buildings in St Leonards, including the Assembly Rooms behind the
Royal Victoria Hotel.

Thomas Brett said the pub was 'owned by my ancestors, the compulsory
removal of which by Governmental orders reduced the owners from gradually
accumulating wealth to comparative indigence [poverty]'.[31] Around 1835 the

pub was dismantled, transported to Shepherd Street in central St Leonards and re-erected as the Foresters Arms, which it is still called today, although it is not now a pub.

Almost adjoining the pub in Trinity Street was a blacksmiths, facing onto Claremont. This and the pub were owned by Thomas Ranger, who was closely related to Brett's mother, whose maiden name was Sarah Ranger. Brett as a youngster worked in both the smiths and the cabinetmakers/pub.

The only other recorded pub on the Ground was the Shipwrights' Arms, which was given a licence in late August 1829.[32]

A notable feature of the Ground would have been its odours. Combating any fresh sea breezes would have been the smell from more than a dozen pig-geries, four slaughterhouses and the Mews's dung pit.

There were many skilled and semi-skilled workers living on the Ground; these are listed in Appendix 3. There is no record of their wages or level of employment, but there were many job opportunities in the rapidly expanding building trade in Hastings, and this was added to when work started on the creation of the new town of St Leonards in 1828. It is likely that many of the Ground's residents were earning their livings in the development of the two towns, so it seems unlikely that the workers would distance themselves from their employers or contractors by seriously declaring independence as a 'new America' (even if they might have liked to).

There is an interesting 'political' parallel between the feeling of semi-inde-pendence among many of the Ground's occupants in the 1820s and the legal

The new town of St Leonards, c.1830.

rights that the Hastings fishermen have today. This is for the fishermen to partly self-manage their section of the beach in front of the Old Town. They had believed for centuries that they had the right to always use that beach on which to work and keep their boats. But in the late 1930s Hastings Council tried to force them to go to Rye so that the beach could be given over to tourists. This was fiercely opposed, and in 1947 a legal agreement was reached that allowed the fishermen to carry on using part of that beach free of charge, indefinitely, and to jointly oversee its management.[33]

Ironically, in the late 1980s the British government introduced tough new fishery regulations, while at the same time the Canadians were relaxing restrictions, so the Hastings fishermen acquired Canadian flags and on one day every boat flew the flag – Canada's, but not the USA's!

5

1827–30: THE INQUISITION

From 1822 onwards there was constant squabbling, and sometimes fighting, among the 'Americans' over who could occupy which piece of the Ground, legally or otherwise. In 1826 these disputes alerted Whitehall to the large-scale squatting that was taking place on a piece of beach that the Crown almost certainly owned. So in late 1827 an official 'inquisition' – a public inquiry – was held by government Commissioners into the legitimacy of what was happening, and this was to result in the 1835 clearance of the Ground.

The *Brighton Guardian* in mid-1828 reported that:

This land [the Ground], within the memory of some of the inhabitants of the town, was sea beach, and was first covered with earth for the purpose of it being converted into a cricket-ground. Portions of it were gradually enclosed for yards and warehouses, cottages etc. About four years ago [*c.*1824], during the rage for speculation, and when land became very valuable, some of the occupiers began to extend their enclosures. This excited a desire in others to become possessed of similar plots of ground; and a general rush was made, especially among the builders, each seizing what they could get, and enclosing it for the purpose of building.

This mode of assumption occasioned several contests, and one building was actually pulled down by Messrs James and Thomas Breeds, two of the old occupiers. It is generally believed that the ill-blood occasioned by violence committed at this period has led to the government claim; and that information has been readily afforded to the Commissioners by those who have thought themselves ill-used, or who were dissatisfied with their portion.[34]

Some of the main feuds between members of the Breeds family ended in Hastings court, as when Boykett Jnr was indicted for violently assaulting his uncle James in October 1826.[35] Occasionally cases were injudiciously carried to a higher court, thus making known to Crown officials the state of affairs, and helping justify their launch of the inquisition.[36]

THE BACKGROUND

The Crown is the manager of all the England and Wales foreshore – the land between high and low water marks – unless some other body has legal rights over it. In 1820 the Crown had become aware of possible problems in Hastings over the Ground, where development was taking place on what had started its life as foreshore up against the *c.*1580 embankment.

So in 1821 the Commissioners' surveyors Albert and Edward Driver had carried out a large-scale survey of what their plan called 'Derelict Land at Hastings'. The available copy of this plan is of too poor quality to reproduce fully, but it does show that by 1821 most of the Ground south of Robertson Street had by then been taken over, with the Breeds being the main occupants.

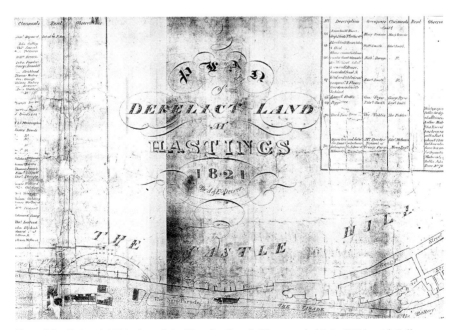

Part of the Drivers' 1821 plan of the 'Derelict Land'. He amended it in 1824, with Pelham Crescent pencilled in (bottom left).

But the marshland north of Cambridge Road was unoccupied, as was the triangle on the west side of Robertson Street, which was called the 'Rock Fair Green' on the plan, with its occupants described as 'The Public'.

Edward Driver returned to look at the 'Derelict Land' in 1824, and in January 1825 wrote on the bottom of the plan: 'Nearly all the vacant ground shown on this plan, except [for the area north of Cambridge Road], has been covered with buildings of various descriptions and by all persons indiscriminately since the plan was made, and without any opposition from anyone.' Driver saw the marshland on the north side of Cambridge Road as a likely target site for the squatters, but this did not happen in the following years.

All the properties on the plan are numbered and described. Not all the written descriptions are legible, but there were about fifty houses, cottages and tenements (possibly a few more), eight gardens, more than a dozen stables, many pigsties, several shops, two slaughterhouses, many sheds and four old boats converted into housing. However, about half the Ground was taken up by the Breeds's shipyard and sheds.

In 1826 the Crown decided they had to do something about this takeover of what was once their land. Had someone else legally acquired it, or did it still belong to the Crown?

An official report by the Commissioners of Woods, Forests and Land Revenues in April 1829 described the background to what had happened.

It said that in 1826 they had decided to establish:

the title of the Crown to a considerable tract of Derelict Land near Hastings, which has within these few years been taken possession of by a number of persons who have erected a great many Houses and other Buildings thereon, without any authority from Your Lordships [the Treasury], or from this Department, for so doing, or paying any rent to the Crown for the ground in acknowledgement of the Crown's title thereto.

The last-mentioned lands adjoin to the town of Hastings, under the Western Cliff, and occupy a space of nearly a quarter of a mile in length and 500 yards in width, which from its situation and appearance was, without doubt, formerly part of the sea shore, upon which the sea in its ordinary tides used to flow and reflow; the Cliff, immediately under which it is situated, bearing evident marks of having formed the ancient barrier against the sea, and of having been in former times overflowed by the daily and ordinary tides; but that by the accumulation of the shingles the sea had gradually receded, leaving the ground in question waste, and for very many years totally unproductive.

The report went on:

> The great increase, however, which has taken place in the population of the town of Hastings, within these 20 years, having created a great demand for Building Ground in the neighbourhood of the town, the land was gradually encroached upon by the erection of Buildings thereon; some under leases, or with the permission of Lord Chichester, who claimed the whole of the ground as owner or lord of the rape or hundred of Hastings, under a Grant thereof in the reign of James the First; and others with the sanction of the Corporation of Hastings, who claimed that part of the land which lies within the liberty of the town, under a Grant made to the Corporation in the reign of Queen Elizabeth; and small rents or acknowledgements were paid to his Lordship and to the Corporation by several of the parties by whom the Buildings were erected.
>
> Having, some years since, received information that by neither of these Grants was the ground in question conveyed either to Lord Chichester, or to the Corporation of Hastings, but that the whole would be found to belong to the Crown, we laid a case before the Law Officers for their opinion, as to the most eligible mode of proceeding for the establishment of the title of the Crown thereto.[37]

The Commissioners were saying that there were two main claims to some form of ownership or control of the Ground: from Lord Chichester and from Hastings Corporation.

The 'Lord Chichester' at that time was Thomas Pelham (1804–86), the 3rd Earl of Chichester. The Pelhams had been one of the most prominent families in East Sussex for many centuries, with several generations entering Parliament. The family had acquired many acres of the county, including three manors and 'hundreds' (administrative divisions) in the Rape of Hastings (the eastern sixth of the county) as a form of grant in 1604 from King James I (king from 1603–25). The Pelhams had bought Hastings Castle and nearby land in 1591, retaining the Castle until selling it to Hastings Council in 1949. The 2nd Earl of Chichester (1756–1826) had started the creation of Pelham Place and Pelham Crescent in front of the Castle in the early 1820s. His son, the 3rd Earl, carried on this work, and also claimed to the Commissioners that King James's grant took in the Ground. But the Commissioners decided it did not.

Hastings Corporation's claim to ownership of the Ground was that it was 'within the Liberty' of Hastings, as was explained in Chapter 3.

The Commissioners' April 1829 report went on to say that 'the ground in question' consisted of two 'parcels', shown as A and B on the report's plan, which had been surveyed early in the autumn of 1827 by Edward Draper, who had carried out the 1821 survey and was to conduct another in early 1829.

Parcel A was 'Old Sea Beach now covered with Buildings', covering 7.31 acres. Parcel B was 1.25 acres of 'Land formerly called Rock Fair Green'. The total area that the Crown was claiming was 8.56 acres (3.46 hectares). The Hastings–Bexhill road, now roughly Robertson Street, was not included in the claim, although after the 1835 clearance the Crown took control of it.

The Crown was also not claiming a fairly small stretch of land along the western edge of parcel B, the old Rock Fair site. On the white space in the map is written: 'Land lately forming part of Cuckoo Hill [White Rock] but which has been cut down and levelled within the last few years.' This space was created by Mark and Boykett Breeds in 1822 by cutting back the hill, as described on page 45, and is now The Alley.

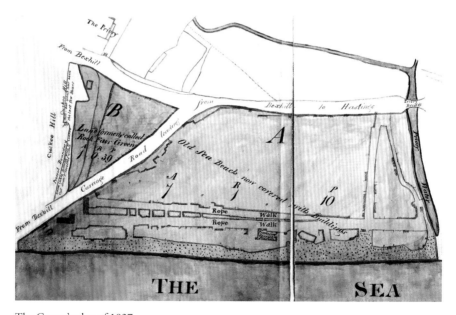

The Crown's plan of 1827.

The Crown could claim the 8.56 acres of the Ground because it was (or had been) beach, over which the Crown had basic rights, but the white space was a former hillside, so it could not be included. However, that space formed about a third of Boykett Breeds Jnr's big multi-purpose storage and work yard, whereas the other two-thirds was on beach that could be included. But the 1835 clearance did not include action on any of Boykett Jnr's yard, leaving it all in private hands. All the yard was gradually built upon over the next four decades as the Breeds sold it off, but with most of the white space (The Alley) being left open. This gave (and still gives) back-access to the new properties on the west side of Claremont, but it created a permanent legal question mark over who was the owner of the space.

THE INQUISITION

In the Commissioners' April 1829 report, which contained Draper's new, more detailed plan (see Chapter 4 page 51 and Appendix 3), they said that they had been advised by their Law Officers to hold an inquisition. This took place on Thursday, 6 December 1827 in Battle, in the George Inn (later the George Hotel), the town's largest tavern. Cynics suggested that the inquiry was taking place in Battle because it was 7 miles from Hastings, a long way away from the possibly trouble-making squatters.

Legally, the inquisition had been ordered by the High Sheriff of the county on behalf of the Crown. An empannelled jury of twelve and three Commissioners heard the various witnesses. About thirty people were at the inquiry. The *Sussex Weekly Advertiser* reported that, 'The proper legal authorities attended upon the occasion, and fully explained to the jury the requisite points of law to guide them in the correctness of their decision.' They duly found in favour of the Crown.

The George Inn, Battle, scene of the inquisition.

The *Advertiser* went on: 'After the conclusion of the business of the day, upwards of 30 of the party sat down to an excellent dinner, and participated in the pleasures of the festive board.'[38] The 'excellent dinner' and 'pleasures' were presumably laid on by the owners of the George Inn, believed to have been the Breeds family.

The claims to ownership by Lord Chichester and the Corporation were dismissed by the jury. The Corporation's four representatives at the enquiry were: Edward Milward Jnr (1765–1833), mayor of Hastings twenty times, who owned land on the east side of the Priory Valley; Frederick North (Hastings MP, 1831–37); John Shorter, who had been mayor on alternate years to Milward; and the town clerk. Brett commented: 'Their representations, however had no weight with the Commissioners, and their claims – if considered as such – were held to have no more validity than those who it was said had illegally appropriated the ground.'[39]

It was also suspected that the Corporation did not actually want to own the Ground, as they would then have to bring under control its thousand or so free-minded residents. The Crown could evict them using military force if necessary, while Hastings Corporation had only a handful of watchmen for maintaining law and order (the Hastings police force was formed in 1836).

Another claimant whose case was dismissed by the jury was Sir Godfrey Webster, owner of Battle Abbey and much land in the Hastings area. He said he was lord of two manors covering much of the Hastings area, and this gave him rights over the land. But his case was dismissed, as nobody had heard of him asking for rent at any time.

It was thought by many of the town's fishermen that they had historic rights to use all of the Corporation's beach, but there is no record of them presenting their case to the Crown in 1827. However, this was a strong feeling that persisted well into the twentieth century, and played a role in forcing Hastings Council in 1947 to give the fishermen legal privileges over the beach, where their boats are today.[40]

CORNWALLIS

The inquisition decided to let the case stay open for six months in order to afford an opportunity for all the affected parties to prove their case.

The person who had perhaps the strongest entitlement to ownership had not actually appeared in front of the inquisition, and does not appear to have pursued his claim in the following six months. This was James Mann (1778–1852), the 5th Earl Cornwallis.

Cornwallis probably had some legitimacy in his claim of possession of at least some of the Ground, as he was owner of three-quarters of the 192-acre Priory Farm. Cornwallis was a former MP and wealthy landowner, whose main residence was the large Grade I listed mansion Linton Park, set in 330 acres 3 miles south of Maidstone in Kent.

The Cornwallis family had bought their part of the Priory Farm in 1764, with the other quarter of the farm going to Edward Milward Snr. The seller had been Henry Pelham-Clinton (1720–94), the 2nd Duke of Newcastle, a powerful figure in British politics. The Duke had strong family connections with the Pelham family, who, in the form of the Earl of Chichester, were to unsuccessfully try to claim ownership of the America Ground in 1827.

The Cornwallis claim was strengthened by a deposition written in 1800 by an 80-year-old former blacksmith, John Lingham, in which he testified that he had always believed that the Ground was part of the Priory Farm. His father Henry Lingham and brother Joseph had rented the farm from about 1750 until 1770.[41]

In addition, a *c*.1750 plan of the Priory Farm Estate shows the *c*.1580 haven and the 'Sea Sands', with the land between them (coloured green here) saying on the original plan: 'This piece of Waste is said to belong to this Farm.'

The 5th Earl Cornwallis inherited the three-quarters of the farm in 1814, but the April 1829 report does not record him putting forward a claim of ownership to the inquisition. The Milwards' quarter of the farm was on the east side of the valley, away from the Ground, but the Earl's section formed the northern frontier of the Crown's claim to the Ground, and, using the *c*.1750 plan, he could have put forward a reasonable case for ownership of part of it, but he did not.

In the decades after the Earl died in 1852 his descendants and relatives, working as the Cornwallis Estate, gradually sold off the Priory Farm for development. In 1864 about 6.25 acres of what had been the *c*.1580 haven

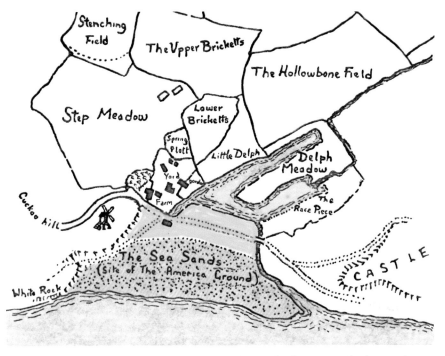

Part of the *c.*1750 plan of the Priory Farm Estate. The windmill is on top of White Rock, and the road next to it is now Dorset Place, with the road across the Valley being roughly Cambridge Road today. (This is a revised copy of the 1750 plan drawn by Barry Funnell, who added 'Site of the America Ground'.)

were levelled, turfed and turned into the Central Cricket and Recreation Ground. It was initially leased to a group of trustees and then sold to them in 1872, remaining a cricket ground until 1994, when it controversially made way for the Priory Meadow shopping centre.

A major scheme for the Cornwallis Estate was the 1873–75 laying out of Cambridge Gardens, on the site of the old Priory farmyard, along with upper Cambridge Road, Cornwallis Gardens and Holmesdale Gardens (named after Viscount Holmesdale, who married the Cornwallis heiress Julia). In 1881 the Linton Road railway bridge, named after the family mansion, was built, opening up the farmland north of the railway for development. In 1885 the Estate trustees built another bridge over the railway, connecting South Terrace to the new Priory Avenue, and donated it to Hastings Council. The Amherst, Braybrooke, Stanley and Wykeham Roads in that area are all named after Cornwallis relatives.

1828 – Notice Served

By chance, while the Crown awaited the result of giving claimants six months' notice to prove their ownership of the Ground, work began on building the new town of St Leonards, a mile to the west.

St Leonards was the creation of London architect James Burton, who had bought what had been farmland from the Eversfield Estate. He decided to build an upper-class seaside resort for the well-off people of London. On 27 February 1828 Burton paid £7,800 (about £850,000 today) for part of Gensing Farm, with a sea frontage of 1,151yd, and the first stone of the new town (the St Leonards Hotel) was laid on 1 March 1828. From 1828 to 1830 he built the seafront (and the Archway at the east end), Crown House, Clock House, North and South Lodges and Maze Hill (west side). The town was built very quickly, and many of the hundreds of labourers and builders employed there lodged in the Ground, adding to the congestion there.

The first shop in St Leonards opened on 5 December 1828, with the hotel opening on 26 October 1829. It was renamed the Royal Victoria Hotel in 1834 following the visit of Princess Victoria to the town that year. 'Burton's St Leonards', as it became known, provided few facilities and houses for the ordinary people that it needed to service the town – builders, labourers, servants, horsemen, shop-keepers, etc. – and in the early 1830s a large working-class suburb quickly emerged on the east side of 'posh' St Leonards.

St Leonards seafront in the 1830s. The Royal Victoria Hotel is on the right.

This became what is now called central St Leonards, with many of its first occupants being the former occupants of the Ground. By 1835 many of them had moved to Shepherd Street, Norman Road, London Road and North Street. The creation of St Leonards opened up a new era in the history of the local building trade, with many builders become rich in the coming decades as all of the borough expanded, because both land and labour were cheap.

On 19 May 1828 notices were served by the Crown solicitor on the Ground's property holders to attend the Court of the King's Bench, there to substantiate their right to any property in their possession. As nobody did so, the government's seizure was made good: the Crown owned the America Ground.

The Commissioners reported in June 1829 that:

In order to obtain possession of this property [the Ground], or a full and complete acknowledgement of the right of the Crown to the same, we proceeded, under the advice of the Attorney and Solicitor General, to cause Declarations in Ejectment to be served upon the different Occupiers.' [The Declarations were notices of forthcoming repossession, by eviction if necessary, and were attached to all the buildings, probably accompanied by the 'broad arrow' symbol of government ownership.][42]

As the immediate resumption of the Property, and the entire removal of all the Occupiers on short notices, would have been attended with great inconvenience to many of them, we have entered into arrangements with a great majority of the Parties, for allowing them to continue, as Tenants to the Crown, for a further period of Seven years, upon such terms as, under the circumstances of their respective cases, seemed to us to be fair and reasonable.[43]

The deadline for the tenants was Michaelmas (29 September) 1835, although in practice they just had to be gone by the end of the year.

On 31 December 1829 the Commissioners reported to the Lords of the Treasury that in the spring of that year they had carried out a detailed survey of all the buildings and their values, in order to decide how much rent the ninety-eight tenants should pay until Christmas 1835. The rents had been agreed with all the occupants.

So the many libertarians occupying the once semi-independent America Ground had become rent-paying tenants of the British government.

The report, published in 1830, said:

> These Rents, it will be seen, amount to nearly one half of the annual value of the Premises; and when it is considered that many of the parties erected Buildings under agreements with Lord Chichester or the Corporation of Hastings, who they believed were entitled to the ground in question, while others laid out large sums in the purchase of these Premises from the original holders, in the confidence that they had a title to dispose of them, the parties have been treated with a proper degree of lenity and liberality, while we shall have succeeded in acquiring, on behalf of the Crown, the undisputed possession, at the end of seven years, of a very valuable Estate, from which no profit or income whatever has hitherto been derived by the Crown.

The survey estimated the total annual value to be £3,072 (£340,000 today), and that the annual rents could be £1,408 (£156,000 today).[44]

But, the report went on to say, only three of the ninety-eight parties (the Breeds brothers) wanted to have formal leases for their premises, while the other ninety-five just wanted to pay the rents that had been negotiated.

James Breeds's property was valued at £690, and a rent of £300; Thomas had premises worth £183, to pay £100; and Boykett Jnr was £60 value and £50 rent. So the Breeds had premises with a total value of £933, being 30 per cent of the total value of the America Ground, and their rent was 32 per cent of the total due.

The report does not record the acreage held by each occupant. However, about a third of Boykett Breeds Jnr's work and storage area (where The Alley is today) was not being claimed by the Crown, and if it were added to the Ground, then the three Breeds would be occupying about a third of the expanded area.

The survey in the report describes each of these ninety-eight tenants, along with details of another thirty named as being tenants of the Breeds.

There is no record of whether the Breeds (or anyone else) actually paid any rent, but the Commissioners in 1829 did not seem to be too concerned about that happening because from 1836 they would have a large piece of vacant and valuable ground that would increase in worth as the town of Hastings expanded.

6

1830–35:
THE LAST YEARS

The 1830s began with an event on the America Ground that symbolised its uncertain future: one of its key occupants was made bankrupt.

Boykett Breeds Jnr (1794–1861) and his father Mark (1774–1828) in 1822 had created a big trade centre on the west side of Claremont, as described in Chapter 3 page 45. In 1824 Boykett Jnr and his uncle Thomas Breeds (1769–1845) bought the luxurious Bohemia House (built in around 1818 by 'Yorky' Smith) and its estate of about 90 acres overlooking the Ground for £12,000, about £1.33 million today. But in February 1830 Boykett Jnr was made

TO NOBLEMEN, MEMBERS OF PARLIAMENT & OTHERS.

VALUABLE FREEHOLD
Mansion and Land, Building Ground, &c.
HASTINGS,
LOTS IV., V., VI. VII. AND VIII. ARE TYTHE AND LAND TAX FREE.

PARTICULARS & CONDITIONS OF SALE
OF A SUBSTANTIAL

Family Mansion,
Newly constructed of White Bricks, with Stone Corners and Window Mouldings, in the Picturesque Style of
AN OLD ENGLISH MANOR HOUSE,
WITH TWO ADVANCED WINGS AND GABLED PARAPETS, AND SLATED ROOFS,
Known as " BOHEMIA,"
RECENTLY OCCUPIED BY H. R. H. THE PRINCESS SOPHIA OF GLO'STER.
TOGETHER WITH
35 A. 2 R. 16 P. OF MEADOW & PASTURE LAND,
It is approached from the Road by a Carriage Drive, at the Entrance of which is a Lodge corresponding in Architecture with the Mansion.
The Out Buildings are of the requisite description, with excellent Stabling and Coach-House.

TWO PIECES OF PASTURE LAND,

Up for sale in June 1832: Boykett Breeds Jnr's estate.

bankrupt, having got out of depth with his expensive property deals, litigation and various misfortunes.

So in 1830 and 1831 most, if not all, of his property (including many houses in Wellington Square and Russell Street) was put up for auction, and the Bohemia mansion and estate was sold in 1832 to Wastel Brisco Jnr (1792–1878).

The Briscos were one of the wealthiest families in the Hastings area. Some of Wastel Jnr's money had come from a slave-run coffee plantation in southern Jamaica, which he had part-owned with his brother, Musgrave Brisco Jnr (1791–1854), when they were young men. In 1834–35 Musgrave Jnr had built the elegant Coghurst Hall on a big estate (now a giant caravan park) 3 miles north of Hastings, and he was a Hastings MP from 1844 to 1854. Their rich father, Wastel Brisco Snr (1754–1834), owned Croft House, the largest house in Hastings Old Town.

A cousin of the two brothers was Sir Wastel Brisco (1778–1862), who owned nearly 2,300 acres (7 per cent) of the island of St Kitts, one of the Leeward Islands in the Caribbean, where he had extensive sugar estates run by slaves. When the British government abolished slavery in 1833 the slave owners received compensation from the British state for the loss of their 'property' – i.e. the slaves. Sir Wastel was given £10,609 (more than £1.27 million in today's money) for losing his 651 slaves. The slaves received nothing.

Wastel Jnr expanded the Bohemia estate, ending up with most of the land on the east side of Bohemia Road as far north as St Pauls Road, plus what are now White Rock Gardens and the Oval. This land remained undeveloped as Hastings spread north and west through the nineteenth century, being a 'green lung' for the surrounding housing estates. Bohemia House became Summerfields School in 1903, but was demolished in 1973 when Hastings Council developed much of the estate by building a fire station, swimming baths, ambulance station, courts and planning offices in a random disorganised manner.

In the early 1920s the widow of a wealthy doctor bought 2¾ acres of the Brisco estate and built on it a private house, which became Hastings Museum and Art Gallery in 1927 when she sold the building to Hastings Council.

The full story of the Brisco family is in Appendix 7.

After Boykett Breeds Jnr's bankruptcy in 1830, his uncle Thomas took over the Claremont trade centre, and Boykett Jnr himself carried on working there in various local trading enterprises, with an office at 67 George Street and a warehouse in Rock-a-Nore Road. Then on 27 July 1861 he committed suicide by drowning at Pett Level, leaving a note in his George Street office saying, 'I cannot exist, my mind is gone.'[45]

Overall, the occupants of the America Ground in the early 1830s seem to have accepted the Crown's seizure of the land in 1828, and they spent their seven years of stayed execution until 1835 earning a living and preparing to move elsewhere in Hastings and in the new town of St Leonards. In April 1830 twenty emigrants left Hastings for the real America, 'a scene which from its novelty at that time excited much curiosity and the expression of many good wishes'.[46]

In June 1832 the new Hastings Improvement Act was given royal assent, giving extra powers to the town's commissioners appointed under the 1820 Improvement Act. The commissioners could have extended the boundaries to take in the America Ground, but instead they stayed away while the Crown sorted it out, and the new Act only applied to the parishes of All Saints, St Clements and part of St Mary in the Castle. Its main purpose was to try and set up a water supply system in those three parishes.

CAPTAIN SWING

The winter of 1830–31 was a significant moment in the history of England, when the 'Captain Swing' insurrection took place in much of the countryside, as many impoverished rural workers tried to stop their employment conditions becoming worse.

Although the uprising began in eastern Sussex and east Kent, and was linked to the widespread smuggling culture, especially in the Hastings area, there is no record of any serious disturbances taking place in the town or on the Ground.

The insurrection had started in Kent in late August 1830, and through the following months the new threshing machines being used by farmers became the main target of destruction. The *Kent Herald* said it was 'a war of poverty against property, of destitution against possession'. On 16 October the radical journalist William Cobbett gave a lecture at Battle, for which he was arrested, but later released. In early November the uprising mushroomed in the Hastings area, and was especially bad around Battle on 3 and 4 November, with barns and ricks being burnt, and a large crowd surrounding the George Inn, where the 1827 inquisition had taken place.

A high-class ball at the Swan Hotel in Hastings High Street on the evening of 4 November ended early, on hearing of the fires. On 9 November farm labourers at Fairlight organised a meeting of all local farmers to demand a wage rise. On the same day, prior to the meeting, the labourers physically removed the Fairlight workhouse superintendent from the parish, with a halter round his neck, never to return. The farmers then thought it best to accede to the labourers' demands, and a decent wage rise was unanimously agreed. Other action in neighbouring parishes also won rises.

An 1830 portrait of Captain Swing getting ready to start a fire.

Over the following weeks Captain Swing spread around much of southern England, but the movement petered out in the summer of 1831. The upper class, however, felt so threatened by the way it had taken place in a seemingly co-ordinated manner, run by a mythical 'Captain Swing', that the government carried out a review of its causes, published in the 1834 Report of the Commissioners on the Poor Laws. Based on information from forty parishes in the Hastings area, the report concluded that:

> Beyond all doubt the practice of smuggling has been a main cause of the riots and fires in Sussex and East Kent: labourers have acquired the habit of acting in large gangs by night, and of systematic resistance to authority. High living is become essential to them, and they cannot reconcile themselves to the moderate pay of lawful industry.[47]

As many of the residents of the Ground were involved in smuggling, they may well have helped the Swingers in their 'systematic resistance to authority', but there is no record of this. The first-ever weekly newspaper published in Hastings, the *Hastings and Cinque Ports Iris*, covered the uprising in detail, but nowhere does it report activity by the 'Americans'.

The 1834 report resulted in the passing of the 1834 Poor Law Amendment Act, which made life much harder for the poor by scrapping the 15,000 parish workhouses (often called 'poor houses') and merging the parishes into 643 unions. Each of these had to build a 'union workhouse', run by a board of guardians. The Hastings board had members from the fifteen parishes in, and close to, Hastings, and in July 1837 the Hastings Union Workhouse opened in Frederick Road, Ore (and is still there). The nearest other union workhouses were in Rye, Battle and Hailsham. The new workhouses, instead of giving aid to the poor, were last-hope places of fear, rather than of help.

Flying the Stars and Stripes

In the summer of 1832 a major political event took place that brought a crowd of 6,000 people to a huge celebratory banquet in Hastings, and another 9,000 to join in the fun and games. This is the only recorded occasion when the flag of the USA was flown on the America Ground.

On 19 July 1832 the banquet was held on the Priory Brooks in celebration of the passing of the parliamentary Reform Bill, which widened the electoral franchise and aimed to make national government less corrupt and undemocratic. The Bill was forced through parliament by the Whig (Liberal) government, which in November 1830 took power from the Tories for the first time in over half a century.

In that month, a Hastings petition said that 'the whole government of the affairs of [Hastings], and of the elective franchise therein, was many years ago illegally and against the freedom of election usurped', and ever since had been illegally kept under the control of 'certain individuals', reported the *Hastings Iris* of 13 November 1830. In its 29 November edition the *Iris* complained that the illegality of what was taking place could have been proved by the town's old records, but 'sacks full of them were burnt not many years since in a neighbouring town'.

Local historian Thomas Brett, then 16 years old, took part in setting up the 1832 celebrations on 19 July, and he described the day's events in his history of the town.

The Priory Brooks in those pre-railway days were the c.1580 haven by another name: the open land between what are now South Terrace on the north side and Cambridge Road on the south, and from Queens Road in the east and Havelock Road/Priory Street in the west. In the month before the revelry £400, the equivalent today of £45,000, was raised to pay for it all.

The 1832 celebrations on the Priory Brooks, where the town centre is today. The Stars and Stripes may be flying above the left end of the building centre right.

Brett said he began work at 3 a.m. on that day, helping to lay out sixty-six large tables in the east half of the Brooks for 'the monster dinner party of six thousand.' Many publican booths, flagstaffs, triumphal arches, a music stage and amusements were set up. At about 6 a.m. a salute was fired from the Castle and church bells were rung, and an estimated 15,000 people began arriving (the population of Hastings was then about 10,100).

A decorated arch had been erected on the Priory Stream bridge, and Brett said the:

bridge marked the western boundary of the old town and the eastern limit of 'America', so nicknamed in consequence of some of the inhabitants forming a settlement in No-man's-land over the (Priory) water. It was here where the formal proceedings of the day may be said to have begun.

At about half-past ten in the forenoon, the town band – augmented for the occasion – headed by a very large procession of 'Americans', who, setting out from the parish of Holy Trinity, passed over the arch of masonry, and under the arch of foliage at the Priory bridge with a very large and handsome banner which they had arranged to present to the Mayor for the use of the town. These Trinitarians, being not strictly under the jurisdiction of the town authorities, had expressed their willingness to join in the celebration upon the condition that they should be allowed to preserve their 'nationality' by carrying an America Ensign in the procession.

Brett went on:

> This condition was not acceptable, it being contended that it would be unpatriotic, if not indeed illegal, to parade the Stars and Stripes without the Union Jack above them. As a compromise, the Union Jack was inserted in one of the corners [of the flag], and a shield with the Hastings Arms in another. There were also other devices and an inscription – 'Presented to the Town and Port of Hastings, by its junior inhabitants, July 19th, 1832, to commemorate the passing of the Reform Bill'.
>
> The loyalty thus displayed was appreciated by the authorities, and the flag was formally received by the Mayor at the Town Hall [on the High Street]. It was afterwards carried with a number of other flags and banners, in procession round the old town, and finally to the dinner field, where the band took up position on a raised platform, and the flags were fixed in the places assigned them. … Thousands of people followed in the wake of the procession, and thousands more came in from other towns and villages.[48]

It is not known what happened to the American flag after 19 July, but Brett described how in the celebrations of the jubilee of Queen Victoria in June 1887: 'The pole on which that banner was mounted was utilised … by Mr Pulford, of St Leonards, for the projection of a flag to signalise the jubilee.' Brett said that the 1832 flag had been 'a handsome silk banner'.[49]

A ROYAL VISIT

Queen-to-be Victoria came to stay in St Leonards in November 1834, when she was 15-year-old Princess Victoria, and her visit prompted changes to the America Ground and its surroundings.

She arrived at a time when serious attempts were being made to join the then-separate towns of Hastings and St Leonards. Prominent local

Dismantling the White Rock promontory in the early 1830s.

businessmen had seen that the two settlements could merge if there were a proper link road under the cliffs. By early 1834 the speculators had already started investing in the future by beginning to cut back the White Rock cliff face, from Robertson Street towards what is now the western end of the line of shops in White Rock. At this time the track under the cliff was officially named as Stratford Place, but all the seafront between Robertson Street and the pier (built 1869–72) was also often called White Rock Place, until being formally renamed as White Rock in 1881.

The high cliff face was stabilised with large-scale brickwork from the early 1830s onwards (much of it still visible), and businesses were being built when possible. These included two big enterprises: Rock's Coach Factory (later Courts the Furnishers), built in 1834–35, and the White Rock Brewery. Also at this time, part of the cliff was cut back at Verulam Place, immediately to the west of today's pier, and ten houses were built there in 1833 or soon after.

By mid-1834 the speculators had made plans on how to complete the cutting back of all of the cliff from Stratford Place to the new town of St Leonards, to both make a decent road and to build housing and businesses on all the newly created ground. This would involve demolition of the remains of the White Rock headland.

However, the sea defence groynes that had just been put up in front of St Leonards were stopping the natural movement of shingle from west to east along the coast, making White Rock and the Ground more exposed to the sea. In the early 1830s a series of serious gales not only caused major damage to many buildings on the Ground, but also cut into the headland and started undermining the first buildings being put up on the White Rock seafront. There were several gales in 1833 and 1834, culminating in a severe storm on 18–19 October 1834 that caused much damage to the Ground, and partially undermined the new businesses at Stratford Place. This generated great fears for their safety, and so temporary sea defences were put up in front of them.

Then, just over a fortnight later, on 4 November 1834, the heiress-apparent to the throne of England came to stay in St Leonards. She travelled from London by road, passing through Hastings en route. But the White Rock coast road had been made impassable by the recent storm, so the entourage had to take the only alternative, a very difficult route via Dorset Place, which had also been damaged by increased use following the breaking up of the coast road by the gales.

The embarrassingly hard time for the royal tour, plus the possible loss of future income through the near-destruction of the coast road, prompted the local establishment to immediately complete the much-needed proper seafront highway between the two towns. But there was a nearly mile-long gap between the official eastern boundary of St Leonards and the western boundary of Hastings, and neither local authority could (or would) pay for an out-of-town project.

The speculators therefore set up a fund to pay for the scheme. Its main investor was Charles Eversfield, whose Eversfield Estate owned much of the St Leonards cliffs, and who hoped to realise a large return from this gamble. The project removed the White Rock headland by blowing it up with gunpowder in the winter of 1834–35, and all the indented cliffs to the west were cut back. The excavated rocks were used to heighten the ground level in front of the cliffs, creating a raised and protected road and parade, running from today's Robertson Street to London Road.

A great deal of property along the Ground's ropewalks was destroyed by storms in January and February 1833, as well as by that in October 1834, when the prominent large house at the west end of the ropewalk was washed away. There was further damage to the Ground and White Rock by terrific gales on 18 December 1834 and 21 January 1835. Eleven small houses on the Ground were swept away by the tide on 21 January. The scale of this destruction was blamed on the sea defences built in front of St Leonards, leaving many Ground occupants with no option other than to move elsewhere – and lots of them went to St Leonards!

A Royal Goodbye

Ironically, a week after the future queen was welcomed to the town by the local people, those of them still on the Ground were served with a notice to quit by the Crown.

On 13 November 1834, notices were received from Mr Driver of the Woods and Forest Commissioners ordering the removal of all the buildings on the Ground before Michaelmas (29 September) 1835, with the end of the year being the informal deadline. Those who complied would not be charged rent for the intervening period, but all property found on the Ground after that date would be confiscated.[50] In theory, the Crown should have been receiving about £1,400 rent annually from the Ground's leaseholders, although it is generally believed that they received little of this.

The combination of this legal order and the damage being done by the sea to the Ground spurred on the exodus in 1835. Many 'Americans' went to St Leonards, where quite a few were already working. They moved into the newly developing area now known as central St Leonards, the land abutting the east side of Burton's St Leonards, especially into Shepherd Street, Norman Road, North Street and lower London Road. This prompted the proper layout and construction of London Road to its junction with Bohemia Road.

Brett recorded that the moving in of the Americans gave an additional impetus to the building operations that had already begun there. 'Fortunately for those [from the Ground] of limited means, materials and labour were comparatively inexpensive at that time, and the dwellings and workshops were run up with but little cost and as little architectural finish.'[51]

Many of the Ground's occupiers took their existing building with them, or, as Brett put it, 'with their houses on their backs'.[52] At least twenty-six houses were built in central St Leonards and White Rock with bits and pieces from the Ground. As many of the movers had probably built their Ground property themselves, they could often be fairly easily dismantled and put together again somewhere else. And if the house had been built using high-quality timber from one of the many shipwrecks along the Sussex coast, it would probably be better to use that rather than other building materials.

Appendix 2 is a list put together by Thomas Brett, with some additions by the late Barry Funnell, of all the properties that were 'transferred', in whole or in part, from the Ground to White Rock and central St Leonards. In addition, it is believed that many Americans moved to the former barrack ground at Halton, and others may also have created some of the line of small houses called High Bank, just north of Mount Road.

Mr Funnell lived in Silchester Road, near North Street, and knew St Leonards very well. In the late 1980s he wrote:

> The best documented transferred house is that known as 'Chapman's', actually a double house, numbers 22 and 23 North Street today. Charles Chapman was the cow keeper on the America Ground who sold milk not only to his immediate neighbours, but was the first daily milk roundsman in St Leonards. His descendants continued to occupy the house until the 1970s.

Chapmans in North Street *c*.1900, and today.

They were keen local historians and had records tracing back their house even beyond the America Ground to the time it stood as a pair of cowmen's cottages on Priory Farm. They claimed that, but for one pane, the glass in the two little bay windows [now removed] had seen life on all three sites. It is truly a house of historical interest.

Incidentally, when the house was transferred to St Leonards, a stall for a cow was built into the basement, and a live cow was kept there to supply fresh milk to special customers living on the Marina. Earlier this century, the cow-stall was converted into a stable for the pony used for the milk deliveries. The approach was from Gensing Road. I mention this use of the premises because it reflects exactly what would have been found on the America Ground – animals living with humans.[53]

In family reminiscences in the *Hastings Observer* of 28 April 1934, Charles Chapman's grandson, also called Charles Chapman, was then running the shop in North Street, selling milk, butter and eggs. He said that in 1834 his grandfather had pulled down the two houses on the ropewalk and had carted them 'lock, stock and barrel to St Leonards, and re-erected in North Street exactly as they were before, even down to the shelves in the shop window'. Grandfather Chapman died while on his round in 1869, and on his funeral procession thirty milkmen walked in front of the cortege.

One of the last buildings to be cleared from the Ground was the Coastguard Station, which had stood roughly where the landward side of the entrance to the Carlisle Parade underground car park is today. It was replaced by a new station in a more commanding position on top of White Rock, on the corner of Prospect Place and St Michael's Place. On 14 April 1836 the first stone was laid, and nine silver coins were put under it, but they were stolen the following night. The new Priory Station, as it was called, is now residences, and still looks much as it did when built. It is the oldest Coastguard building in the Hastings area. The old station was taken down and the new one built by Mr Clement, a draper by trade.[54]

The only surviving relic of the pre-1836 America Ground that is still in situ and visible today is the Breeds-family cliff face behind Claremont, with one or more of the caves in it, although it is not known which. The sandstone cliff face was stabilized in 2021 as part of the major changes to the *Observer* building, and the caves were improved and made more useable.

7

1836–49: THE DESERT

From 1836 till the end of the 1840s most of the cleared Ground was an open space of grass, sand, mud and some left-over odds and ends. Officially it was called the Crown Land, but it was also semi-officially known as the Government Ground, the Priory Land and the Priory Ground. However, locally it was 'familiarly spoken of as the Desert', said Brett.[55] It was also unofficially called the Priory Desert, the Derelict Land, the No-Nation Ground and the Waste Land. And then during the 1840s it would start becoming known as the America Ground.

Ironically, at the end of 1835, at the very moment the Crown took possession of the Ground, the Hastings establishment was forced by law to scrap the elitist way it had been running the town and had to set up the new Hastings Council, which had powers over the very land that the Hastings Corporation had done its best to keep at arm's length for many decades. Following the radical parliamentary reform of 1832, the Whig government had passed the 1835 Municipal Corporations Reform Act to bring similar improvements to the structurally corrupt local government system in urban areas.

Hastings was one of 178 boroughs listed as being run by a handful of money-making and unrepresentative individuals, with a tiny electorate. An enquiry was held in the town in February 1834 into the working of the Hastings Corporation, and its report said that: 'For a long series of years the entire corporate control of the corporate body was in the hands of Mr Milward, an opulent neighbour.'[56]

The 1835 Act reformed the 178 corporations by establishing a uniform system of municipal boroughs, governed by town councils elected by ratepayers. The boroughs had to publish financial accounts and set up a police force. Councillors were elected for three years, and the councillors (not ratepayers) could elect aldermen for six years. Until 1835 Hastings had been run by the Hastings Corporation, a small group of people whose legal basis for doing so was the 1589 Charter. The new Act was passed on 9 September 1835, and the first Hastings election was held on 26 December, with the reformed Hastings Council came into being on 1 January 1836.

The town was divided into two wards: East (the parishes of All Saints, St Clements and St Mary-in-the-Castle), with twelve councillors, and West (all the other parishes as far as St Leonards, a separate town), with six councillors, plus there were six aldermen.

So instead of the western boundary of the town being the Priory Stream, which had been the Corporation's aim, the Act extended the new council's responsibilities westward as far as St Leonards, taking in the Ground.

THE LATE 1830S

From 1834 to 1839 a cloud of uncertainty hung over the Ground as the Hastings Corporation and then Hastings Council tried to raise funding for a harbour to be constructed in front of the town, but this came to nothing and the scheme was abandoned.

Meanwhile, the Commissioners of Woods and Forests had to do something to protect their Ground from the increasing encroachment of the sea following the cutting back of the White Rock headland in 1834–35. A survey of the Ground was carried out by Walker and Driver of the Commissioners, with the help of George Thwaites of the local shipbuilding family, and they recommended erecting a stone wall along the seafront.

Hastings Council backed the idea in mid-1836,[57] and in December that year the Council had its own survey carried out by local surveyor John Banks.[58]

Entitled 'A plan of the public roads through the Holy Trinity Ground westward of Hastings', it shows that there was still one building standing on the America Ground: a 'blockmaker's shop etc'. This is the rectangle centre-right on the plan. It had been making rigging as part of James Breeds' shipyard.

It stood on the 'Road to the beach', at the top of which, on the left side of its junction with what would soon become Cambridge Road, is a tiny square. This is labelled the 'Toll House', and was erected by the Crown in 1828 as the place where their many tenants on the Ground could pay their rents over the next seven years, but its coffers apparently remained almost empty.

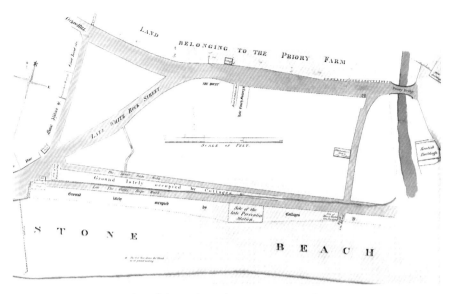

Hastings Council's 1836 plan of the roads on the America Ground.

Today's Robertson Street is described on the plan as 'Late White Rock Street', while Claremont is not named. On the west side of Claremont are the Breeds family's 'Lime Kilns etc, Carpenters' Shops etc, Coal Yard etc', having escaped the 1835 America Ground clearance.

The words 'Stone Beach' are between two red lines, and on the plan, in very small writing, it says that that area was still beach. Below the northern red line is 'Ground lately occupied by cottages', and it was along the seaward edge of this that the sea wall was built.

In 1837–38 the Commissioners had the wall constructed by Hughes and Hunter of St Leonards. The *Cinque Ports Chronicle* newspaper of 15 September 1838 reported that there was a 'Parade' on top of the wall, 'formed of a composition of adhesive clay, covered with the sweepings and cuttings of Portland stone etc, which will ensure an excellent promenade'.

It was said to be the best wall of its kind along the coast, and its wall formed a strong sea-defence for almost a century, until the construction of the Carlisle Parade underground car park in 1930–31. This was Britain's first underground car park, and the historic wall survives in good condition, being the inland wall on almost the whole length of the inside of the car park, and it can be easily seen.

But without sea defences the Ground was still flooded. The *Brighton Gazette* of 12 November 1840 said:

The new sea wall, *c.*1838 – and it is still there!

> The late storm having converted what in summer was a sandy desert into an extensive lake by the waves breaking over the Parade, and covering a considerable portion of the Government ground, the ordinary paths and communication for foot passengers to St. Leonards has been … cut off, persons being obliged, after wandering through a labyrinth of heaps of rubbish from the demolished Priory Houses, to adopt a circuitous road.

A picture of the sea wall appeared in the national news magazine *The Illustrated London News* of 4 May 1844 when a small steamship called the *Waterman* was nearly wrecked on the beach in front of the sea wall.

The magazine reported that:

> On Saturday afternoon [30 April] this gallant little craft met with the following serious accident off Hastings. … She arrived at Hastings about half-past two, and in passing the town unfortunately too near in shore, struck on a dangerous reef off the Priory, known as the Castle Rocks, which she passed over and injured her bottom. It being found that the water was flowing fast into her, she was put about [turned round], and run on the sand off the Parade, where she filled as the tide flowed, and at high water the hull was covered. A quantity of empty casks were slung round her during the evening, by means of which she

was got further in, and on Monday she was pumped out, and had her leaks stopped. She has since floated off, and been removed opposite the Priory stade for the purpose of undergoing repairs.

The accompanying drawing is interesting, as it shows some sheds on the Ground, while other pictures and accounts from 1836–50 describe the area as empty. On the far right is the new Cambridge Road, with the Breeds' lime kiln chimney in Claremont next to it. On top of the

The *Waterman* runs ashore on the America Ground in May 1844.

hill is the Coastguard Station and its signalling flagpole.

During the discussions in 1836 with the Commissioners of Woods and Forests about building the sea wall, Hastings Council had suggested that the Crown could carry out other improvements to the Ground, including setting apart an open space on the Ground for public use, while a harbour still seemed possible.

In June 1836 the Council wrote to the Commissioners saying that in the old days the Ground 'served as a place for the inhabitants … to play at cricket and other games requiring space, and for the fishermen to dry nets, and contributed in a great degree to the advantage, health and convenience of the said town and its inhabitants. That a public fair [the Rock Fair] was moreover from time immemorial held thereon on the 26th day of July annually.' But in 1836 the land was 'derelict and waste', the Council said, and there was no place for amusements or exercise in the open air requiring space in Hastings; nor was there any level ground accessible for such purpose except that at the Priory.[59]

But the Commissioners replied that there was no Act of Parliament that gave them the power to grant the land for that purpose.

However, they agreed that it would be good to remove the 1822 Priory Bridge and lay the stream in a large iron culvert to drain the Priory Brooks into the sea. The pipe would be covered over, thereby linking the Ground

The cleared America Ground in the early 1840s, after the Priory Stream had been culverted and the scene set to become the new heart of Hastings. On the left is the Priory Coastguard Station, built 1836, with some officers keeping an eye on things. The large building below them is the coach and carriage factory of Rock and Son, who exhibited at the 1851 Great Exhibition.

with Hastings and creating new ground for general use. A hurricane on 29 November 1836, which destroyed Brighton's Chain Pier, brought heavy flooding and damaged the Priory Bridge, highlighting the need to both build the sea wall and remove the bridge.

In November 1838 a tender for £916 was accepted, with the Crown paying £400 of it.[60] Earl Cornwallis was asked if would increase his contribution of £100, but he 'sent a letter of refusal, commenting somewhat bitterly on the injustice of the rating on his property, the Priory Farm'.[61] The culvert work was carried out between November 1838 and April 1839. The area on and around the culvert was surfaced and levelled, creating the open space that became the heart of the town when the Albert Memorial clock tower was built roughly on the site of the bridge in 1863.

The new culvert improved the drainage of the marshland that had been too wet to build on, following the construction of the big embankment in about 1580. From 1839 developers started contemplating the marshes and the future potential of the many acres.

THE NEW ROADS

From 1836 to 1839 two different groups of business people built rival turnpike roads to improve the town's communications with London, with one abutting the Ground.

The founder of St Leonards, James Burton, wanted a more direct route to London than via Hastings, so he was the leading force behind the creation of today's London Road, Sedlescombe Road South, Sedlescombe Road North, a bridge under the Ridge and the A21 from there to Whatlington, where it connected with the existing Hastings–Flimwell turnpike road. But the owners of the Flimwell road were worried that Burton's road could lead to the loss of trade in Battle, so they upgraded Cambridge Road and Bohemia Road, and created Battle Road from Silverhill through to Beauport. All these roads played a key role in shaping the layout of much of the north part of the borough as it is today.

But the coming of the railways in the 1840s quickly spelled financial disaster for the new roads, a failure that the St Leonards backers tried to avert by obtaining in 1841 one of the last-ever turnpike acts from Parliament. They had already built a branch road through Sedlescombe to Cripps Corner, the B2244, and the 1841 act allowed them to extend this to Hawkhurst, from where travellers could reach Staplehurst on the London–Dover railway line.

The new Cambridge Road – then called Bohemia Road – opened in mid-1838. In the town centre, it was built several yards to the north of the old Hastings–Bexhill Road, making it a straight line from the Priory Bridge (which was still in place when the road was laid out) to the junction with Dorset Place. From there a new roadway was cut through the slope of the hill. Until then traffic going to Battle and London from the bridge had to go up Dorset Place, along today's White Rock Gardens, and then turn right into White Rock Road. The new turnpike road created today's route, missing out Dorset Place, and creating a smooth slope all the way from the town centre to the top of Falaise Road.

The part of the new Cambridge Road from the bridge to Dorset Place was also much higher than its predecessor as it passed Claremont. Until then the old road was on the same level as Claremont, and traffic could go from Claremont round to Dorset Place. The difference in height can be seen in the flight of steps from Claremont into Cambridge Road.

The old Hastings–Bexhill Road was the northern boundary of the America Ground that the Crown had taken over in 1835. But the new Cambridge Road,

View from the Castle about 1840. The bottom of the newly created Cambridge Road can be seen, raised up on the spoil from the cutting up the hill. Most of the Breeds's large trading centre in Claremont is still there, having survived the 1835 clearance of the America Ground.

as we know it today, is to the north of that old road, so, strictly speaking, what has usually been thought to be the northern boundary of the America Ground is not Cambridge Road, but the backs of the properties in Trinity Street, and then the pavement on the south side of Robertson Street going into the town centre.

The creation of the good quality new turnpike roads drew attention to the poor state of the Bexhill road as it crossed the America Ground, being little more than a wide, lumpy footway. After many complaints about the deplorable conditions on the Ground in general, the Commissioners and Hastings Council began serious discussions about the road in 1840.

Brett commented that in 1840: 'For five years the Ground had been a rough, sandy, shingly and limey desert, in the very heart of the borough, over which her Majesty's mail passed with as much safety only as could be ensured by manageable horses in the hands of vigilant and careful drivers.'[62] The *Brighton Gazette* said the Ground was in a 'disgraceful state', with 'a labyrinth of heaps of rubbish from the demolished Priory houses'.[63]

The 1841 national census recorded just nine people living in the Holy Trinity parish, and these were probably all connected with the Priory Farm, so there were probably none on the Ground. In the 1831 census there had been 1,074 people in the parish, in 1821 there were 294, and 76 in 1811.

In May 1848 a long-lasting leftover from the pre-1836 days was described in a letter in the *Hastings News* complaining about the large amount of dust blowing around the 'desert land'. The correspondent said that halfway across the Ground 'there is a little *oasis* which remains green and flourishing in the driest seasons, even when all around is dry and bare. This *oasis* marks the spot upon which stood the manure-heap of the Pelham Mews. Although 13 years have elapsed since the Mews was pulled down, and the soil consists of little else than gravel, or beach, the effects of the manure are still visible.'[64]

Although the site of the Ground was still a desert in 1848, at least the Bexhill road-cum-footway had been improved by then. This was the result of the discussions that began in 1840, and resulted in August 1841 with the Council deciding to press ahead with the scheme. A Council meeting in early 1843 heard that the recently laid-out new track-way – Robertson Street as we know it today – had cost £150, towards which the Commissioners had contributed £100.

But there was still no lighting of the road, despite the lengthy negotiations over its site. The problem was that installing gas lighting between York Buildings and White Rock would be expensive, and would have to be paid for by the ratepayers in the parish. But there was only one ratepayer in the Holy Trinity parish, Mrs Foster at the Priory Farm, and this was seen to be too unfair, so the lighting problem remained in the dark.

The Commissioners had taken their time in agreeing to the location of the road because, as Edward Driver of the Commissioners said in 1840, 'I consider much depends on it to enable us to dispose of the Crown Land to the best advantage.'[65]

When the Crown took control of the Ground in 1836 it was not clear what that 'best advantage' could be. The heart of Hastings was still the Old Town, and the new St Leonards was based around the Royal Victoria Hotel, almost 2 miles away. Both towns were steadily expanding towards each other, making the Ground a likely place for profitable development, but on the other side of Cambridge Road the Priory Valley was still marshy farmland, a doubtful site for expansion of the borough. A widespread theory in the late 1830s was that the Crown was leaving the Ground empty and unused while it waited to see how and where the town would grow, and therefore what value their land would have.

Train Time

The Commissioners were given a good incentive to bide their time in the early 1840s when it became known that the rapidly expanding national system of railways was heading in the direction of Hastings. The first line to reach the

LONDON & BRIGHTON RAILWAY.

OPENING OF THE RAILWAY

FROM

HASTINGS

AND

ST. LEONARDS

TO LEWES,

BRIGHTON, AND LONDON.

ON AND AFTER

SATURDAY, JUNE 27TH INST.,

The following Trains will start from the Temporary Station,

BULVERHYTHE:--

At 7 a.m., arriving in Brighton at 8.30, in time for the Express Train for London.

9.45 a.m.,	"	Brighton at 11.20,	London at	1.30.
12.15 p.m.,	"	Brighton at 1.50,	London at	4.
5 p.m.,	"	Brighton at 6.50,	London at	9.30.

FROM LONDON AND BRIGHTON FOR BULVERHYTHE:

London at 7 a.m., arriving in Brighton at 9.30.,	Bulverhythe at	11.10.
London at 11 a.m., " in Brighton at 12.30 p.m.,	Bulverhythe at	2.10.
London at 12, " in Brighton at 2 p.m.,	Bulverhythe at	4.
London at 5 p.m., (Express) in Brighton at 6.30,	Bulverhythe at	8.10.

Full Particulars will appear on the Time Bills.

	Express.	1st Class.	2d Class.	3d Class.
Fares between Hastings and London	15s.	13s.	9s. 6d.	6s. 6d.
" Hastings and Brighton.		6s.	4s. 6d.	3s.
" Hastings and London, (Day Ticket)	22s. 6d.	20s.	14s.	9s. 9d.
" Hastings and Brighton, (Day Ticket)		9s.	6s. 9d.	4s. 6d.

LONDON TIME WILL BE OBSERVED AT ALL THE STATIONS.

First, Second, and Third Class Carriages will be attached to all the Trains between Hastings and Brighton.

London, June 18th, 1846.   *T. J. BUCKTON, Secretary.*

CREASY AND BAKER, GAZETTE OFFICE, BRIGHTON.

The town's first trains, 27 June 1846.

borough – from Lewes – arrived on the outskirts in 1846, and by 1852 there were three lines – heading west, north and east – that were all served by the new Hastings railway station in the Priory Valley. This quickly turned the southern part of the Valley into the Hastings town centre, and the Ground – less than a quarter of a mile from the station – suddenly became a very valuable piece of real estate.

Work began on the Hastings railway services in early 1846, and a temporary station was put up at Bulverhythe, just to the east of the Bull Inn on Bexhill Road. The first public service train arrived there at 11.20 a.m. on Saturday, 27 June 1846, and there were celebrations around the town, including bell-ringing and the firing of guns. The line was being built by the London, Brighton and South Coast Railway (LBSCR), and it was extended in November 1846 to the new West Marina Station (now gone), a few yards west of the Bopeep Inn. This was the nearest station to Hastings until the Hastings Station opened in 1851. The railway was immediately successful because of its superiority over road transport. Even the fastest stage coach took seven hours to London, while in 1849 LBSCR introduced a special express train that reached it in two and a quarter hours.

South Eastern Railways (SER) – a rival company to the LBSCR – was given Parliamentary permission to build the next line, continuing the LBSCR line from Bopeep through Hastings and Rye to Ashford. SER also obtained power to build a line from Tunbridge Wells to Bopeep, but only on condition the Bopeep–Ashford line was completed first.

SER started work on the Ashford–Rye section of the line in 1846, but there were delays on the Rye–Bopeep portion until February 1849, by when the piece from Ashford to Rye was almost complete. There were major problems from Bopeep: two long tunnels, an embankment across the Priory Valley, then two more tunnels to the other side of the Ridge, followed by a downhill gradient with a series of embankments and cuttings.

Work on the two tunnels, from Bopeep–Warrior Square and Warrior Square–Hastings, was completed at the end of 1850, using 16 million bricks, enough, if loaded into trucks, to form a train 22 miles long. The spoil from the tunnels was spread on ground and marshes near their entrances, creating land on which were built Havelock Road, Cambridge Gardens, much of Cornwallis Terrace, Devonshire Road and the top of Middle Street. This added to the lifting of ground level immediately to the north of the Ground when Cambridge Road was created in 1838.

In the east, a huge embankment was laid across the Priory Valley and two tunnels were dug: under Mount Pleasant Road to the Ore Valley, and then under the Ridge. All this work was more or less finished by December 1850, and the Bopeep–Ashford line – and Hastings Station – officially opened on 13 February 1851, with the two companies sharing the station.

So in 1851 there were two indirect routes to London, via Lewes and Ashford. But SER's Tunbridge Wells–Bopeep line would be a shorter option, and work

The new Hastings Station (top right) soon after the opening of the Tunbridge Wells line. Havelock Road and Station Road have been laid out, and building work is under way in Cambridge Road. From the *Illustrated London News*, 14 February 1852.

was carried out while the other two lines were being built. The 27 miles of the Tunbridge Wells line opened on 31 January 1852, but another sixteen years were to elapse before the more direct line was completed with the opening of the Tonbridge–Lewisham route via Sevenoaks. Initially there was no station at Bopeep on the Tunbridge Wells line; the West St Leonards Station was built there in 1887 to serve the westward expansion of St Leonards.

The arrival of the railway in west St Leonards in 1846 and the plans for the Hastings Station to be sited close to the Ground must have given the Crown Commissioners great hope for a profitable leasing of their still-empty waste land. On 27 December 1848 they reminded everyone that they owned the Ground by closing the road across it from 11 a.m. to 4 p.m. The *Hastings Chronicle* reported that: 'A man was stationed at each of the entrances to the ground [at York Place and White Rock], to see that the order was not infringed, and the entrances were further blocked up with hurdles, on which hung boards containing the announcement.' But 'the order was in general readily obeyed', and the parade along the sea wall was left open.[66]

This ownership reminder by the Crown was a forerunner of their lease of the Ground in the following months to a successful Scottish businessman – and future Hastings MP – Patrick Robertson, whose wealth had been built on selling opium to the people of China.

8

THE 1850s: THE ROBERTSON GROUND

By 1850 the 8½ acres of the Crown Land had also started to become known as the 'America Ground', but perhaps it should have then been called the 'Robertson Ground', for most of it had been leased from the Crown by the wealthy Scottish businessman Patrick Robertson, who was embarking on a large-scale development that was to transform the area. The large open space, which less than two decades previously had been covered in temporary homes, sheds, workshops, stables and pigsties, was to be transformed into a high-quality residential and shopping district.

The arrival of the railways from 1846 and the siting of the Hastings Station in the fields of the old Priory Farm quickly turned the Priory Valley into a new town centre for Hastings. Robertson saw this was going to happen, and in early 1849 he signed a deal with the Crown for a ninety-nine-year lease of the Ground, which was going to be close to the station that was to become the town's travel hub.

Patrick Francis Robertson (1807–85) had started making his fortune by selling opium to the people of China in the late 1820s and '30s. He was born in Meigle, Perthshire, the eldest son of the Reverend Daniel Robertson, Professor of Oriental Languages at the University

Patrick Robertson.

of St Andrews, in Fife. He had a well-off uncle, Robert Small, who lived partly in Hastings, and Robertson got to know the town in the 1820s by visiting him.

In 1826 the 19-year-old Robertson emigrated to Calcutta and then went to live in Canton in China, working for his uncle's trading companies that made large profits from selling Indian-grown opium to China via Canton, the only Chinese port open to foreign traders. The highly addictive opium was causing the deaths of many people, and the Chinese government said the dealings were illegal. Their attempts to stop opium being imported culminated in the Opium War of 1839–42, which Britain won, to the financial benefit of Small, Robertson and other traders. The minor Chinese port of Hong Kong was given to Britain, and when the war came to an end, Robertson bought the largest available section of its development ground.

From the early 1840s onwards, although Robertson was effectively living in Britain, he became involved in the management of several London-based international banking and insurance businesses, especially in the Far East, including China.

In 1847 he moved to Hastings, buying the attractive detached villa called Halton House, which stood in a large garden in Halton, looking down the Bourne Valley to the sea. The arrival of a rich businessman was to transform the America Ground – and the town of Hastings.

The full story of his life is in Appendix 6.

THE PLAN

Patrick Robertson was a member of the Conservative Party, and he stood as its candidate for Hastings in the August 1847 general election, but was unsuccessful, and he then seemed to cast his thoughts on the development potential of the America Ground. He appears to have quickly struck a deal with the Crown, because historian Thomas Brett said that in April 1849 'brick-making was commenced in a field near the hop gardens (now the Alexandra Park) to be used in the erection of the mansions on the Government Ground'.[67]

Paying £500 a year for his lease, Robertson took possession at a special event on Friday, 8 February 1850. The *Hastings News* reported: 'The ceremony of transferring the Crown Lands from Her Majesty's Commissioners to its future proprietors took place on the spot, by each party providing a representative, the gentleman appearing on the behalf of the Commissioners conducting the other over the lands. This ceremony of "walking in" completed the transfer.'[68]

Being a shrewd businessman, Robertson had employed the Crown architects Messrs Reeks & Humbert, of 7 Whitehall Yard in London, to produce plans that would be acceptable to the Commission, whose office was just round the corner from them, in Whitehall. The architects set up a temporary Hastings office at 15 Pelham Crescent, moving to Carlisle Parade when it was built.

Their outline plan was of 'Houses etc to be erected on the Crown Estate, Hastings (as approved by the Commissioners of Her Majesty's, Woods, Forests, etc). To be carried into effect from the design and under the superintendence of Messrs Reeks & Humbert, architects.'

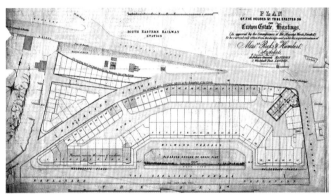

The 1850 plan.

The plan showed that the area to be developed was in three sections:

1. the south side of Robertson Street and all the land between there and the seafront, taking in the west side of Harold Place;
2. the north side of Trinity Street and the two Robertson Street properties adjoining it;
3. the triangle formed by Robertson Street, Claremont and Trinity Street.

Not included were the west side of Claremont, and the north side of Robertson Street from the Congregational Church eastwards, as they were not part of the Crown Estate.

The plan also depicted large 'Assembly Rooms' on the corner of Harold Place and Robertson Street, but these were never built.

Buildings that came later, and are not on the plan, are the Holy Trinity Church, built in 1857 along the south side of Trinity Street, and the large

Queens Hotel (now the Queens Apartments) on the corner of Harold Place and Robertson Terrace, built 1859–62. Eight houses are on the plan for the site of the Queens Hotel.

Parts of the seafront were originally going to be named after a prominent local family, the Milwards. What is now called Robertson Terrace was shown on the plan as Milward Terrace, with the terraces on the seafront at both ends called Waldegrave Place. These names were in recognition of the Countess Waldegrave, inheritor of the extensive Milward estates, who was a generous benefactor of many needy causes in the town.

The whole of the seafront from Robertson Street to Harold Place (on the plan called Harold Street) was an elegant roadway called Carlisle Parade, being named, possibly diplomatically, after Lord Carlisle, the First Commissioner of Woods and Forests when Robertson's lease negotiations took place. The name Waldegrave Place was dropped, and the two terraces were (and are) called Carlisle Parade.

All of Carlisle Parade had been built on ground raised to the height of the 1836 sea wall, but the wall stopped when it reached where the west side of Harold Place is today, so the Parade terminated there, several feet above Harold Place, meaning Carlisle Parade was not a through road. It was the rebuilding and widening of the seafront in the early 1930s that lifted the seaward end of Harold Place to meet Carlisle Parade, thereby turning the whole seafront into the busy A259.

The Crown Estate's 1851 view of how the 'houses now in the course of erection' would look.

THOUGHTS OF THE NEWS

The pro-Liberal *Hastings News* of 15 February 1850 gave its thoughts on Robertson's proposals:

> It is … with no small degree of pleasure that we now offer a remark or two on the plan for the proposed buildings to be erected on the Priory Ground.
>
> Many of our readers, doubtless, recollect the 'Desert' (as it has recently been denominated), ere Neptune and the Board of Woods and Forests combined to give a stimulus to local emigration by rudely disturbing aboriginal right, and by a fearful *duo* of 'ruthless waves' and 'Royal edicts' violate the sanctity of many a homestead and destroyed the 'local habitation' of many who now reside in other parts of the neighbourhood, and who, at the period of which we write, might have sung his native air, 'Home, sweet home!' while wending his way by the dwellings of his corporate-trammelled neighbours to free 'America,' and knew:
>
> *By the smoke that so gracefully curled*
> *Above the Rope Walk, his cottage was near.*
>
> But this antique accumulation of ill-built and undrained houses has long been removed, and we do not grieve the change. The ground has for the last few years presented a waste, a 'bleak and sterile wilderness': a fact which needs not our pen to awaken it in the recollection of anyone who has chanced to journey across it on a winter's day, during a gale from the north, with snow, rain or hail as an accompaniment.
>
> A scheme is now in working for covering the ground with capacious mansions and shops, which, when erected, *may* become again the homes of those who were driven from their 'native land' to wander in the strange country (ie, the towns of Hastings and St. Leonards) by their enemies, the allied powers (waves and Commissioners).
>
> We have inspected the plans for the intended buildings, now lying at the office of Messrs Reeks and Humbert. A row of neatly-built residences of good size is intended for the sea front. This will consist of 36 houses, the frontage of each being 22ft 6in, and the depth 40ft.

The centre houses will be run back in the form of a crescent, the space in front of this crescent being filled up by a grass plat or pleasure-ground. The line of frontage will be 70 feet from the sea wall (and we believe it is intended to erect another groin in the vicinity of this wall). A carriage road and promenade will be allowed in the front of the houses here.

The plans show the buildings to be neat and plain, so far as external architecture goes. This is a trait in accordance with the spirit of the time, which will not sacrifice the useful to the decorative. If the sections laid down for the interior are carried out, we believe that comfort and accommodation will be the result. … This place will, in all probability, be the *heart* of the borough.[69]

1850–51

Patrick Robertson's basic plan for his development was that Robertson Street and Trinity Street would be shops, while the sea-facing Carlisle Parade and Robertson Terrace would be residences and hotels. Building leases would be for ninety-eight years, to 1948, with Robertson himself first of all creating the necessary roads, footpaths and sewers.

Robertson advertised for construction bids even before he legally took possession of the Ground. An advert in the *News* of 25 January 1850 sought tenders by 11 February from 'builders, contractors and others … to construct forthwith the roads, vaults and sewers' of the 'Crown Lands'. The sewers would be built with '1,125 feet of glazed stone-ware pipes of 18-inch bore'. They would have drained onto the beach opposite.

Ironically, four days after the sewer tenders were due in, an important inquiry began at Hastings town hall into the state of the sanitation in Hastings. This was part of a national investigation set up by the Public Health Act 1850 following the cholera epidemic that had swept the country in late 1849. There was no single drainage system in the borough, and the eleven-day inquiry found widespread deplorable conditions, especially in the Old Town. An inspection of 'lodging houses for tramps etc' in All Saints parish found several were in:

a very unhealthy condition. Many of these wretched hovels had no privy at all – without drains, without everything that would add to the health and comfort of the miserable inhabitants. The universal practice was the use of a bucket in which they emptied their slops, and which was kept in a sort of cupboard, and the contents were occasionally emptied in the sea. In the vicinity of these places there are other habitations, not lodging houses, which may be said to be in an equally disgusting plight.

The inquiry found that a particular problem was the way 'liquid manure' was discharged onto the beach along the seafront, as Robertson was presumably going to do.[70] It was not until 1866–68 that a large-scale sewage and drainage system was set up, with a storage tank and discharge outlet at Rock-a-Nore (which is still there).

The *News* of 8 March 1850 reported that: 'Active building operations have been commenced upon the waste land at the Priory. Workmen are briefly engaged laying the main drains, and forming the foundations and cellars.'

The first stone of the western block of Carlisle Parade was laid at 11 a.m. on Monday, 24 June 1850. 'Having performed the interesting ceremony,' said the *News* of 28 June, 'the parties retired to the Wellington Inn [at 43 White Rock], to partake of a *dejeuner*, a band of music playing several lively airs, much to the gratification of the assembled multitude.'

Construction of some of the buildings took place quickly from then onwards, starting with this western part of Carlisle Parade and with the eastern end of Robertson Street.

Robertson was probably spurred on through 1850 by the rapid completion of Hastings Station and the railway lines in the Priory Valley. On 7 September the first-ever railway engine to arrive in Hastings was carried into the Valley by road from Bopeep on a large carriage drawn by sixteen horses. Named *Samson*, it was put on the lines and began 'puffing' on 9 September, initially helping with the construction of the Mount Pleasant tunnel through to Ore.

The south side of Robertson Street was developed steadily, and on 4 October 1850 the first shop opened on the Ground: Mr Henry Polhill's pork butchery at No. 4 Robertson Street, where the HSBC bank is today at the east end.

However, the north side of Robertson Street lay undecided on the drawing board for some time.

1852

Hastings Council in early 1852 published a large-scale plan of Hastings (but not St Leonards). This shows that by then all the south side of Robertson Street, plus the west end of Carlisle Parade and the first three properties at the west end of Robertson Terrace, had been completed. But the north side of Robertson Street, Trinity Street and the east side of Claremont had not been started by then, and neither had the majority of Robertson Terrace and Harold Place.

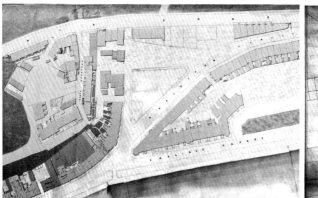

Part of the town's 1852 survey. The plan on the right was completed later than that on the left.

However, the 1852 plan also shows that development was under way in several places just outside the boundaries of the Ground:

- On the section of the north side of Robertson Street from Trinity Street eastwards.
- On the west side of Claremont. The southern half had been built on by 1852, but the northern half was still occupied by the Breeds yard and buildings, dating from 1822 onwards. Boykett Breeds, the owner declared bankrupt in 1832, was still running the establishment, 'being a lime-burner, as well as a coal, timber and porter merchant'.[71] He died in 1861.
- On the south side of Cambridge Road. This had not been claimed by the Crown at the 1827 inquiry because it had been a well-established roadway for over two centuries. It is not known who had the legal right to sell or lease it for the development that was shown to be well under way in 1852.

By June 1854 Carlisle Parade and the west end of Robertson Terrace had been completed.

The 1852 plan shows nothing for what we know today as the north side of Trinity Street, but it has an outline sketch for the 'Trinity Triangle': the south side of Trinity Street, the east side of Claremont and the north-west section of Robertson Street between these two roads. In early August 1851 Reeks and Humbert had advertised for contractors to lay out this triangular portion of the estate. 'The works comprise the formation of the roads, including granite curb, channelling and surface drainage; also about 400 feet of 12-inch glazed stone-ware pipes, forming a main sewer.'[72]

1853–57

Two large statues had been erected on pedestals at either end of the wall in front of Robertson Terrace's grass open space by late 1853. At the west end was a lion, and at the east a unicorn (both still there). These were created by sculptor James George Bubb for the major redesign of Buckingham Palace that was completed in 1847, when the eastern Pall Mall frontage was constructed.

It is believed that the 4.2m-high statues had been intended for the Palace's reshaped forecourt, but were not used, and they were then acquired by Decimus Burton, the architect of the new town of St Leonards, who had planned the new entrance lodges and the railings surrounding the Palace. Historian Barry

Funnell believed that Burton 'transferred them to the Department of Woods, Forests, etc, for use at the Hastings site to indicate Crown ownership'.[73]

The lion and the unicorn are heraldic symbols of the United Kingdom, appearing in the royal coat of arms. The lion stands for England and the unicorn for Scotland, and the combination therefore dates back to the 1603 accession of James I of England, who was already James VI of Scotland. The plinths have carved floral panels on three sides.

Construction of numbers 4–12 Robertson Terrace, parallel with the seafront, took place from 1852 till early 1854. Numbers 1–3, on the terrace's south-east facing curve, had already been built by 1852.

But in the spring of 1854 George and James Winter, the local builders of numbers 4–12, went bust before they had completed the work, and the nine attractive high-quality houses were auctioned that summer. The cause of their bankruptcy is unknown, but it is likely that they (and Patrick Robertson) had been overly optimistic about the market for luxury properties in a town that had not yet felt the benefit of the improved communications that the new railway service would bring.

By the time of the 15 July auction, numbers 4–7 Robertson Terrace had been finished and let at annual rents payable to Messrs Winter of £160 (£18,000 today), plus an annual ground rent of £20 (£2,250) to Robertson. But numbers 8–12 were not completed, with the auction advertisement saying they were 'substantially built and nearly finished'.

All five of numbers 8–12 were described as having in the basement:

housekeeper's rooms, servants' hall, footman's room, spacious cellars with detached kitchen and scullery. On the ground floor, spacious hall, dining room, library, and butler's pantry. On the first floor, front and back drawing rooms, handsome stone staircase to second floor, back staircase ditto front, front and back bedrooms, dressing rooms, and two water closets. On the third floor, front and back bedrooms, and dressing rooms with closets, and also a three stalled stable, coach house, and coachman's apartments.[74]

The details of numbers 4–7 in an earlier advertisement are similar to those of numbers 8–12, but without stables, coach houses and coachman's apartments.[75]

It was the bankruptcy of the Winters that probably resulted in the terrace remaining uncompleted for several years, as shown in an 1855 photo and on the

The east end of Robertson Terrace in 1855, still undeveloped. On the left is the unicorn statue.
The black sheds are on the estate; the buildings behind them are on the east side of Harold Place
(most now gone).

1859 plan (page 107). Missing in 1859 were four more houses facing the sea,
plus another three on the terrace's south-west-facing curve. Eventually, most
of the sea-facing terrace became the big Albany Hotel, which was effectively
destroyed by a bomb on 23 May 1943, killing eleven Canadian soldiers billeted
there. The buildings either side of the hotel were also seriously damaged, and
eventually much of the terrace had to be demolished. Today, only numbers
1–6 are the original early 1850s buildings. Between number six and the Queens
Apartments are the Albany Court flats and the former Debenhams.

Robertson Terrace was not the only part of the Ground being less successful
than had been hoped. In March 1857, numbers 1, 4, 5 and 11 Carlisle Parade
were advertised in the *Sussex Advertiser* as being for sale, plus numbers 28, 29,
30, 31 and 39 Robertson Street, and 3 Robertson Terrace.

Patrick Robertson was warmly thanked by Hastings councillors in November
1856 when he presented them with a large gold badge to be worn by the future
mayors of the town. Weighing 98g, the 18-carat gold badge has the town's coat
of arms in hand-painted enamel, surrounded by oak leaves. Robertson at that
time was MP for Hastings, and in 1875 his successor Thomas Brassey donated
the chain on which to wear the badge. Both are still worn by the mayor today.

Churches

Today, a prominent building on Robertson Street is the Holy Trinity Church, occupying about three-fifths of the triangle. It was built 1857–58 but originally it had been intended to site it outside the America Ground.

Following a public meeting on 5 April 1855, the Reverend G.D. St Quintin of St Leonards asked the Woods and Forests Commissioners if a church could be built on the undeveloped triangle, but they refused. However, the trustees of the neighbouring Cornwallis Estate offered the Reverend half an acre of ground for a very small price, and he accepted.[76] This is where numbers 15–18 Cornwallis Gardens are today, close to the junction with Cambridge Road.

Work began in late November 1856, but almost immediately there was a landslip, and the architect, Samuel Teulon (1812–73) said the site had to be abandoned.

The Cornwallis Estate had no other ground available, so the land on which the Holy Trinity Church now stands had to be bought from the Crown for £2,500 (£285,000 today).

The laying of the foundations started in early 1857, and on 22 July that year the foundation stone was laid on one of the corners by the Countess Waldegrave, the main funder of the church. Mr Teulon was the architect, and

The laying of the Holy Trinity's foundation stone on 22 July 1857.

the builder was the well-known local contractor John Howell. The church opened on 29 September 1858, but it was not consecrated until April 1882 because it took until then to pay off its debt.[77]

A drinking fountain in honour of Countess Waldegrave was opened on the corner of Trinity Street and Robertson Street on 24 May 1862 (and is still there, but without water). This was the first public drinking fountain erected in Hastings and St Leonards.

The construction of Holy Trinity had received £200 funding from Lady St John (Louisa Boughton). She was concerned that many of the poorer working-class people who in the early 1830s had had to move from the America Ground to central St Leonards did not have an appropriate church there, as the two existing St Leonards churches charged pew rents and were patronised mainly by wealthy residents and visitors.

So Lady Louisa paid the entire cost of building Christ Church on the site of a quarry in London Road, opposite Kings Road. It was built with stone from the quarry, and was free of pew rents. It opened on 9 September 1860, and quickly became so popular that it was decided to build a much bigger church on vacant ground on the corner of Silchester Road, adjoining the existing church. The foundation stone of the new Christ Church was laid in November 1873 and it was dedicated in May 1875. The first Christ Church is now a community services centre.

The Holy Trinity Church is the only church standing on what was the America Ground, but in 1857 a much smaller church was built just outside the Ground's northern border, on the south side of Cambridge Road.

This was the Congregational Church, replacing the nonconformist chapel that had been built in Croft Road in 1805. It was enlarged in 1864, and then was demolished and replaced in 1885 by the current, much larger building, designed by the local architect Henry Ward and built by John Howell. It was then known as the Robertson Street United Reformed Church, and its main entrance was (and still is) in Robertson Street, with its southern edge on the America Ground boundary.

1858 ONWARDS

In January 1859 Hastings Council published the first-ever large-scale map of all the borough. It had been surveyed by the Borough Surveyor John Laing

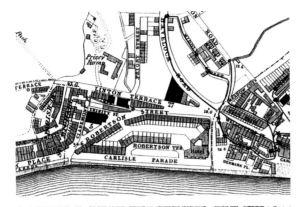

Above is a Hastings Council map of 1859, and below is a 1938 Ordnance Survey map. Both have a red line (drawn by the author) showing the boundary of the land leased to Patrick Robertson in 1849. Linton Terrace in the 1859 map is Cambridge Road.

in 1858, and it gives a detailed picture of the town in that year. The section covering the town centre is shown here. It is believed that this is a reproduction of a copy that was used by Laing or one of his staff to record the town's new drainage system, shown by the thick black lines drawn in many streets.

The 1859 map shows that by 1858 most of what was the America Ground had been fully developed. The only unfilled spaces were the west end of the north side of Trinity Street, some of the west side of Robertson Street close to the Holy Trinity Church, and the east end of Robertson Terrace, where the former Debenhams and part of the Queens Apartments are today. The Apartments are the converted Queens Hotel, construction of which had started in 1859, and is shown on the map. It opened in 1862. It had originally been planned to have large houses here.

On the west side of Claremont, which was not Crown land, the 1859 map shows that the northern half of it was still what had been the large general-purpose yard of the Breeds family. They had started selling parts of the yard from at least the 1840s, while still occupying it until development took place.

An 1867–68 street directory lists numbers 1–10 of Claremont as being built and occupied, with the rest of the west side as 'Manner and Winter, general smiths; Barham, Wm, painter, plumber, etc; Winter, George, coal merchant'.

In this former Breeds yard, major changes took place from 1870 onward. In that year No. 12 Claremont was built (its site had been sold by the Breeds

in early 1849 when Patrick Robertson began preparing to lease the Ground).
No. 12 is a striking five-storey building, next to Hastings Library. Part of it was
rented by Frederick Parsons (1844–1900), owner of the *Hastings Observer,* and
local entrepreneur Henry Cousins, who together set up a printing works there.

The 1873 Ordnance Survey plan (below) shows the last surviving part of
the Breeds yard just before it was developed. The large red-coloured building standing in a large open space is probably their warehouse, with the space
giving access to the long grey structure to the west. It is not clear what this was,
but the northern section of it may be a big cave cut by the Breeds family in the
1820s, probably as a storage depot. Today the eastern half of the sub-basement
of the *Observer* building occupies that site.

The plan shows the gap between the rear of Claremont and Prospect Place
(now known as The Alley) much as it is today. There are several caves along
The Alley, one or more of which possibly date from the days of the America
Ground, and, if so, are the last surviving relics of the Ground still visible.

The *Observer* became so successful that soon after 1873 Parsons bought all
these remains of the Breeds yard, and in 1877–78 he and the wealthy Thomas
Brassey (1836–1918) combined to build both the Brassey Institute (today's
Library) and No. 14 Claremont, the 'Parsons Steam Printing Works'.

Brassey had inherited a fortune from his father Thomas Brassey (1805–70),
who had built 5 per cent of the world's railway mileage at the time of his death.
The free reference library, on the ground floor, was opened by Brassey in January
1881. It was his gift to the town, along with all the books, and he was letting
the Hastings Rowing Club use
the basement to store their craft.
Brassey was knighted late in 1881,
and in 1886 was rewarded with
a peerage for his public services.
In 1890 he helped set up the
Hastings and St Leonards Museum
Association, which was based in
the Institute until it moved to
John's Place, where it is today. In
August 1895 the first Hastings
Chess Tournament was held in the
Institute, and it was so successful
that it became an annual event.

The north end of Claremont in 1873.

After all of the *Observer*'s locally based newspaper rivals closed down in Edwardian years, Parsons built a new headquarters for his printing and publishing business at 53 Cambridge Road, while retaining usage of No. 14. Details of the history of the *Observer* are in Appendix 9.

In 1885 No. 12 Claremont became the home of the first Hastings telephone exchange. The first English exchange had opened in London in 1879, but the new communications system only spread slowly round the country because of strict government restrictions. These were relaxed in 1884, and the newly formed South of England Telephone Company opened an exchange in No. 12 in the spring of 1885, probably on the top floor. In 1894 the service moved to 47 Cambridge Road, which today abuts Rock House. The phone companies were nationalised in 1912, coming under the Post Office, and the exchange in 1930 moved to the big new Post Office premises built on the corner of Cambridge Road and Priory Street.

In late 1858 a locally owned limited company built the 'Hastings and St Leonards Central Assembly Room and Arcade' between Robertson Street and Havelock Road, shown in black on the 1859 plan, with the number 27 below it. The Assembly Room, also called the Music Hall, was the upper floor, holding 800 people, while the Arcade was ten shops on the ground floor, with extensive cellarage in the basement. The upper floor was renamed the Public Hall in mid-1883, as it was by then being used for many purposes. Charles Dickens lectured there in February 1884, and in later years it became the Orion Cinema. Today the building is Yates pub.

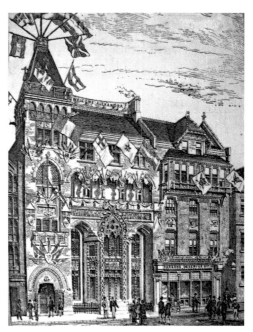

The newly built Brassey Institute and *Hastings Observer* printing works (on right) welcoming Princess Alexandra to the town for the opening of Alexandra Park on 26 June 1882.

The last remnants of the Priory Farm, the descendant of the medieval priory that had dominated the Priory Valley, were removed and its land built on in the early and mid-1870s. The development was between Cambridge Road and the railway line, creating Cambridge Gardens, Cornwallis Gardens, Cornwallis Terrace and Holmesdale Gardens, plus the south ends of Linton Road and Braybrooke Road.

In the years immediately before the First World War the suffragette movement had a strong presence in the Robertson Street area. The suffragettes were campaigning for votes for women, and the term refers in particular to members of the Women's Social and Political Union (WSPU), a women-only movement founded in 1903 by Emmeline Pankhurst, which engaged in direct action and civil disobedience. A Hastings WSPU branch, commonly known as the Militants, was set up, and in early November 1911 it moved into the shop at 8 Trinity Street. This was its headquarters, depot and meeting place, but it soon proved to be too small, so in late June 1912 the Militants moved into the ground floor of 8a Claremont. When the war began in 1914 most suffragettes moved away from suffrage activities and focused instead on the war effort.

Another national political movement that appeared on the former America Ground in Edwardian years was the Independent Labour Party (ILP), which was affiliated to the Labour Party, but was further to the left. On 3 January 1910 the Hastings branches of both the ILP and the Church Socialist League opened the 'Socialist Literature Depot' at 51 Robertson Street, close to the junction with Cambridge Road. In the run-up to the general election on

Early January 1910: Left-wing Labour campaigners outside their Robertson Street depot in the run-up to the 1910 general election.

15 January, the purpose of the Depot was 'instructing the electorate on the true aims and objects of socialism'.[78] Discussions were held every evening at 8 p.m. Unfortunately, there was no Labour or ILP candidate in the election, which was won by the sitting Tory MP Arthur Du Cros.

The day 26 September 1927 saw the opening of the 'Hastings Palace of Industry' – the new Plummers department store (later Debenhams). The *Hastings Observer* described it as 'The New Mecca for Ladies', with 'the ground floor entirely devoted to all the delightful fancy goods that are a necessity in every woman's life'.[79] Plummer Roddis Ltd had demolished their existing buildings and created what was to be the town's leading department store from then onwards. It was designed by Hastings architect Henry Ward, who died the same month that Plummers opened. Debenhams closed on 3 May 2021.

The biggest change to Robertson's 1850s America Ground was the reclamation in 1931 of a further 60ft of the foreshore to create Britain's first underground car park, and at the same time to lay on top of it today's A259 main road. This was part of the rebuilding of most of the borough's seafront by Borough Engineer Sidney Little in the 1930s. Until then Carlisle Parade had been a no through road, as at the east end it was several feet higher than Harold Place. Mr Little had raised the height of Harold Place at its seaward end.

The ninety-nine-year lease of the Ground to Patrick Robertson ended in 1948. The Crown retained ownership and acted as landlords until 1995, when the Ground was sold to a

Above: July 1908: The staff of Plummer Roddis being taken on their 'beano' – the annual trip to a pub out in the countryside for food, drink and games. Below: The new Plummers, later Debenhams, opening in September 1927. The building behind the tall post in the labove and on the far right of the 1927 picture is the HSBC bank.

Building the underground car park and new road in front of Robertson Terrace in 1930–31. The wall behind the drill is the former sea wall, which today is the north wall inside the car park.

newly formed London company called Fivecourts Ltd, which took out a mortgage with the Midland Bank.

LAST WORDS

Journalist and historian Thomas Brett, who had known the America Ground through its key years, recalled in the 1890s:

If those who were ejected from the Hastings 'America' were at all cognizant of how the money comes and goes by Government hands, they might well have felt sad – as some of them did – that they had invested their savings, as they thought at the time not improperly, in the erection of cottages or workshops, from which they were afterwards to be driven, to seek a home and a living elsewhere. But, as it's an ill wind that blows no one good, so there came a time, tardy as it was, when instead of the ill-assorted and irregular lines of the Priory property there stood in their place the handsome houses and shops now existing, probably to the benefit, and certainly to the improvement of the whole borough.[80]

Robertson Street in 1863.

APPENDIX 1

THE GROUND'S NAMES

What is now known as the 'America Ground' was sometimes called 'America' in the 1820s and early 1830s, but there is no record of the name 'America Ground' being used before 1848, although it may have been. The name meant the Ground that had once been America.

In the 1848 book *A Ramble about Hastings and St Leonards*, the author Alex Crux referred to the 'American ground' (without a capital 'g'), while in a court case the *Hastings News* of 30 June 1848 reported that 'a miserable looking female, whose appearance certainly bore no testimony in her favour', and who was 'extremely importunate and troublesome', was jailed for seven days for begging on the 'America ground' (again, no capital 'g').

Names of the Ground used before the 1835 Clearance

America
No Man's Land
The Outlands
The Priory
The Priory Ground

The Priory Land
The Shingles (in the eighteenth century
    mainly)
Squatter-Land
The Squatters Colony

Names of the Ground used immediately after the 1835 Clearance

The Crown Estate
The Crown Land
The Derelict Land/Lands
The Desert
The Government Ground
The No-Nation Ground
The Priory Desert
The Priory Ground

The Priory Land
The Waste Land

APPENDIX 2

HOUSES AND BUILDINGS TRANSFERRED

The list below is of buildings that were transported in whole or in part from the America Ground and re-erected elsewhere in the borough. Most of the details of this list were put together by Thomas Brett, with other entries by Barry Funnell.

There are many central St Leonards houses that have been built using beach stones, but none of these properties seem to have been moved from the America Ground.

London Road

19   South corner of South Street. Brought by John Tyhurst.

27   Now called Chinese Town. Brought by Edward Picknell.

Norman Road

33 and 35   Destroyed by bomb (were next to the Warrior Gate pub hit by bomb). Brought by Stephen Milstead, a plumber who had four houses on the America Ground.

37 and 39   The shop now numbered 33 was probably originally 39. Brought from the ropewalk by Joseph Naylor, who had several properties on the America Ground.

57   House with bay front – the largest transported from the Ground. Brought from where Yates is today in Robertson Street.

North Street

11   Brought by Mr Milstead.

12 and 13   Brought from the ropewalk by John Foord Snr. There is a passage between them.

22 and 23   On south corner of Gensing Road. Brought from the ropewalk. Owned by milkman Charlie Chapman; see story on page 80.

Shepherd Street

2   The Foresters Arms. It was the Black Horse pub and its adjoining property, standing where the north corner of Trinity Street and Claremont is today.

6 and 7   Brought by Mr Milstead from where Holy Trinity Church is.

10 and 11   Brought by Mr Hammond, of Bexhill.

28, 29, 30   Brought by the Wellerd family; James Wellerd later became the Hastings gaoler and was murdered in 1856.

White Rock

22–26   It was probably on the ropewalk terrace; brought by the brothers William and John Austin.

42   Possibly transported, plus maybe another one or two small houses.

Halton

There is no record, but it has been said that some houses were moved there, and/or possibly to nearby High Bank.

APPENDIX 3

THE AMERICAN PEOPLE

These are the details of every person named in the 1829 Crown survey.

The first list is of all the people who had made agreements to pay rents to the Crown, apart from the Breeds brothers – James, Thomas and Boykett Jnr – who are detailed after this list.

This list shows the tenant's employment, the annual value of their premises, and a description of the premises.

The value of the premises is given in pounds sterling, with '*s*' meaning 'shilling', twenty of which were in the pound. A pound in 1829 would be worth about £111 today.

'B' means brick-built, 'T' timber-built, 'BT' brick- and timber-built.

Austin, John	Carpenter	£65	5 B tenements in a brick house
Austin, William	Confectioner	£70 8*s*	3 houses + offices adjoining
Avery, Edward	Labourer	£10 8*s*	B house
Baker, Charles	Carpenter	£16	B house, yard
Ball, James	Wheelwright	£8	Enclosed yard
Bassett, Elizabeth	Widow	£5	B house, garden
Beard, Francis	Labourer	£49 8*s*	3 B houses, yard
Bowmer, Edward	Block/mast-maker	£10	T cottage, yard
Bowmer, Joseph	Mast/block-maker	£30	B cottage, shed, timber yard
Brazier, James	Shoemaker	£20	2 B houses
Brazier, Mary	Widow	£40	B house, 2 other buildings
Brazier, William, Jnr	Postman	£10	B cottage
Brazier, William, Snr	Shoemaker	£12	Cottage, stable
Breach, Wm, John & Mark	Fishermen	£12	Chaise-house, stable, piggeries
Bumstead, Daniel	Servant	£10	Stone-built tenement
Chester, Samuel	Baker	£38	T Cottage in 3 tenements
Cobbey, Thomas	Mariner	£10 8*s*	Cottage
Colvin, Laban	Baker	£32 10*s*	3 BT houses, yards
Coopper, Dennis	Fisherman	£10	T cottage, small yard
Crisp, Sarah	Widow	£56	Cottage, stables, offices, building

Cutting, Samuel	Carpenter	£14	Neptune Cottage, shed
Daly, John	Servant	£26	2 B houses, yard
Day, Peter	Grocer	£6 16s	T tenement, T shop
Eaton, John & Ben Standon	Carpenters	£27 16s	Cottage, saw lodge, yard, workshop
Elphick, John	Labourer	£14 6s	Stone-built house, garden, shop
Fowler, John	Labourer	£1	Enclosed yard
Fowlers, Elizabeth	Widow	£11 14s	BT house, yard
Freeman, John	of Ashby, Kent	£2 12s	B house
Gallop, John	Shipwright	£34	Several tenements, yard, piggeries
George, George	Labourer	£16	2 stables, shed, yard
Golding, Thomas	Mariner	£12	B house, yard, shed
Hall, William	Servant	£26	BT cottage, forecourt
Hammond, Mary	Widow	£32 10s	2 B houses, blacksmith's shop, forge
Hayes, James	Servant	£55 6s	2 BT houses, yard, school room, stable
Hayward, Samuel	Miller	£43 11s	2 cottages, warehouse
Hilder, James	Miller	£28 18s	2 houses, garden
Honiss, William & Edward	Cabinetmakers	£20	T House
Howell, John	Gardener	£4	T cottage on wheels, canvas roof
Hutchings, James	Servant	£7 16s	B tenement
Hyland, George	Labourer	£20 16s	T house, yard
Hyland, James	Labourer	£18 14s	2 BT cottages
Hyland, William	Carpenter	£28 12s	T cottage in 4 tenements
Keen, Richard	Servant	£45 16s	Double cottage, B house
Lansdell, James, of Battle	Builder	£30 4s	B house, yard, stable, slaughterhouse
Lively, Joseph	Coachman	£20	BT house, stable, yard
Longley, William	Tax collector	£19 10s	2 B cottages
Lulham, Richard	Labourer	£18 4s	BT house
Lusted, Thomas	Carpenter	£60	2 B cottages, 1 tenement, sheds, yard
Mann, James	Fisherman	£6 10s	B house
Mann, Thomas	Fisherman	£33	2 B houses, garden
Mannington, John	Shipowner	£20	Blacksmith's forge

Manser, Mary Ann	Widow	£10	BT cottage
Masters, Moses	Shipwright	£29 18s	2 T houses, garden, forecourt
May, John Dean	Shipwright	£5 4s	T cottage
Merrix, William	Labourer	£28 12s	2 B cottages, gardens
Milstead, Stephen	Plumber	£75 16s	4 BT houses, slaughterhouse
Murdock, Mary	Widow	£8	B cottage
Naylor, Joseph	Gentleman	£44 4s	Several T cottages, small buildings
Naylor, Joseph	Lodging housekeeper	£35	T cottage, garden
Osborne, Lesy	Labourer	£1	T stable, yard
Page, Thomas	Rope maker	£33	2 B houses, wash-house, garden
Paul, Edward	Mariner	£12	T house, yard
Picknell, Edward	Carpenter	£26	2 cottages, yard
Picknell, William, Jnr	Carpenter	£9 2s	B dwelling
Picknell, William, Snr	Carpenter	£36 14s	3 houses, stable, yard
Piper, William	Fisherman	£18 4s	B house in 2 tenements
Prior, John	Brewer	£24 14s	2 B tenements, wash-house
Ranger, Thomas	Shoemaker	£14 16s	Blacksmith's shop, another shop, loft
Robinson, James	Labourer	£10 8s	B and stone cottage
Smith, Edward	Porter	£75	3 cottages, other small buildings
Smith, John	Builder	£10	B mason's shop, yard
Squires, Thomas	Butcher	£20	3 slaughterhouses, piggery, shed
Squires, William	Butcher	£3	Yard, slaughterhouse
Standon, Ben & John Eaton	Carpenters	£27 16s	Cottage, saw lodge, yard, workshop
Stevens, Edward	Livery stable keeper	£16	B house, small yard
Strickland, George	Corn factor	£20 16s	2 B houses, yards
Surden, Samuel	Rope maker	£18 4s	2 B cottages, yard, piggery
Swain, John	Fisherman	£18 4s	BT cottage in 2 tenements
Thatcher, Henry, of Battle	Gentleman	£7 10s	Cottage, yard
Thomas, Daniel	Publican	£27	2 T cottages, yard
Thorne, Thomas	Bricklayer	£20	B house

Thorpe, Thomas	Ostler	£12	B house, yard
Thwaites, Henry	Grocer	£15 12s	B house, yard
Thwaites, Thomas	Gentleman	£33	Rope warehouse, coal sheds, stables
Tyhurst, John	Brewer	£34 2s	2 houses, garden
Vine, William	Bricklayer	£12	B cottage
Waters, Thomas	Sawyer	£8 16s	T cottage, yard, shed
Wattey, Ann	Widow	£6 10s	B house
Wellerd, James	Carpenter	£48 2s	4 houses, offices
Wellerd, William	Butcher	£35	Several stables, large yard, piggeries
Weller, Henry	Baker	£3	Bakers-house, yard
West, George	Carpenter	£10	T house, yard
Wood, Ann	Widow	£3	T shop, shed, yard
Young, Edmund	Carpenter	£39	3 B tenements, offices

James Breeds

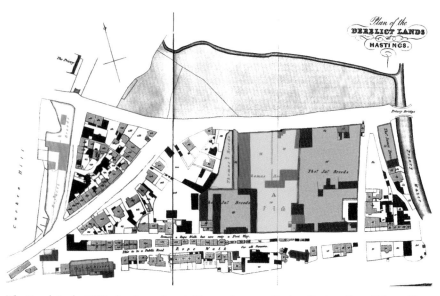

The Breeds in the 1829 plan. James in red, Thomas in green, Boykett Jnr in yellow. Coloured by the author. The original plan, in a larger format, is on page 8, the frontispiece.

James had a very large yard (on the right-centre in the plan) whose tenants included William Ball, Messrs Winter and Wingfield, Robert Bowmer, Ransom and Ridley (shipbuilders) and John Austin. James also had the Pelham Mews (in centre), the base of the town's main coach service, run by Edward Stevens, who had his own house roughly where Trinity Street is today.

In other parts of the Ground, James also had some housing, including a terrace at the west end of the ropewalk, where lived Mary Aylesbury, Edward Bridger, Mrs Bridger, Thomas Brisenden, John Kent, Mrs Morphee, John Prior, John Roper and Samuel Sinden. At the east end of the ropewalk was what the 1829 report called 'A small tenement, formerly an old boat, or part thereof. Occupier: Late Henry Tilden.'

James's best-known property was a large boat called the *Polymina* (below the large yard). It was described as 'An old hulk, now in two tenements. This old brig was brought here 22 years since [ie, 1807], and was then the first house on the property (except Mrs Brazier's house on the Mount), and both the present tenants lived in the brig when it was first brought.' The tenants were Thomas Page and John Prior.

James's premises had an annual value of £690, for which he agreed to pay £300.

Between James's Pelham Mews and his very large yard there was an equal-sized yard occupied by his brother Thomas.

Thomas Breeds

Thomas's tenants were William Beeney, William Kennall, James Kock, James Lansdell, William Standing and Thomas Thorn. Thomas Breeds also had a fairly large piece of open ground on the other side of the Pelham Mews, let to the Mews manager Edward Smith.

Thomas's premises had an annual value of £183, for which he agreed to pay £100.

James Lansdell (also in the main list, above) was married to Thomas's daughter Martha, and he built Breeds Place, the terrace of six large houses adjoining the west end of Pelham Crescent, completed in 1828. While doing that, he was helping build the first house in St Leonards, 57 Marina.

Boykett Breeds Jnr

Boykett Jnr had a large piece of the Ground, occupying all the land on the west side of Claremont coloured yellow in the plan. Its annual value was £60, for which he agreed to pay £30. There is no record of him having any tenants. He also owned the adjoining land, within the lineage, but this was not being claimed by the Crown.

In the 1829 survey, the area is under his father's name, Mark Boykett Breeds, but he had died in May 1828.

Emigrants

These are people who are known to have moved from the America Ground to other parts of Hastings and St Leonards. The ones marked with an X are also in the 1829 lists above.

Barden, Thomas		Neve, Charles	
Beaney, Thomas		Noakes, Stanton	
Chapman, Charles		Prendegast, J.	
Chapman, Edmund		Pulford, J.	
Chester, Samuel	X	Russell, William	
Fitzgerald, Mrs		Savage, George	
Hyland, James	X	Shaw, William	
Kirby, William		Shepherd, Robert	
Lee, George		Sinden, Henry	
Levett, Valentine		Sinden, Samuel	X
Milstead, Stephen	X	Starnes, Richard	
Morris, –		Strickland, William	
Murdoch, James		Thorne, Thomas	X
Naylor, Joseph	X		

APPENDIX 4

THOMAS BRETT

Thomas Brandon Brett was born in George Street, Hastings, in a house backing onto the Light Steps (with a garden), on 30 May 1816, to Thomas Brett and Sarah Brett (born Ranger). He had eleven siblings. His father had been a blacksmith who in late 1826 took up fishing instead. On 26 November 1826 he was found dead in a fishing boat, of which he was part owner, on the beach opposite the Cutter Inn. The *Sussex Weekly Advertiser* said (4 December): 'He had often been in the habit of distancing himself from his home, and sleeping on board his boat.' He died from arsenic poisoning (possibly suicide).

As a result, from a very tender age Thomas had to act as the support of his widowed mother and help in the house, and in the care of his brothers and sisters. In 1828 his mother, Sarah (*c*.1792–1831), married a Mr Woolgar, a builder, and Thomas was sent to Mr Neve's school in Bourne Street. He had only a year and a half at school before leaving to assist his stepfather.

In 1831 Thomas became an errand boy in the draper's shop Messrs Clement and Inskipp, near the Fishmarket, for three and a half years, at 4*s* (20p) a week. The hours of business were from 7 a.m. to 9 p.m., and often later. In his dinner hour he would run to help the men in the smithy, which was on the America Ground, where the west end of Trinity Street is today.

The 1829 Government lease for the smithy went to Thomas Ranger, probably a brother of Thomas Brett's mother. Next to the smithy were the buildings of William and Edward Honiss, cabinetmakers, which were converted into possibly the only pub on the America Ground at that time, the Blacksmith's Arms. Thomas Ranger also owned these premises, and Brett says he worked in both sets of buildings at one time.

He also learned to mend and make his own clothes, and during the cold winter of 1833 he began to write poetry, and he started the study of music.

From 1837 to 1839 he worked for the post office in George Street, rising soon after 4 a.m. to take in the mail, and working there till 10.30 at night. The kindly old postmaster, Mr Woods, taught him to knit shawls and make tables and chairs. His tool chest at that time contained a hammer, a chisel without a handle, a broken carving knife, an old plane and a gimlet.

Thomas Brett.

Then in 1839 Brett set out for America, but the weather was bad; he had an accident and damaged his spine, and was landed at the Spithead. He returned to Hastings and that autumn he moved into 66 Norman Road, St Leonards. Then he started a small school on his own in Market Terrace, behind Norman Road and near the St Leonards Archway. He was a persuasive teacher and took great pains with the boys, and for a time was requested to take charge of the National School in Mercatoria, which he carried on concurrently with his own school. In January 1844 he married Celia Barden (1823–1900), and it was a happy marriage.

Brett then started a new chapter of his life, a more public one. He established the first brass band to play on the Parade in the evenings and on holidays, as well as a string band much in demand for soirees and entertainments. In 1848, with Philip Hook, he helped to establish the St Leonards Mechanics' Institution, being elected treasurer in 1853, a position that, with that of president from 1888, he held for very many years.

He had a great reverence for the power of the press, and acted as correspondent for the *Sussex Weekly Advertiser* from 1839. Then in 1854 he bought his own printing press and started *The Penny Press* as a monthly. The following year he commenced the weekly *St Leonards & Hastings Gazette,* managed entirely by himself from his home in Norman Road. He might be seen in the mornings running up and down the steps of the leading lodging houses, collecting the names of the visitors; later in the day he would compose his leaders, often setting up the type as he thought out the subject. He also took part in the actual machine work of printing, and finally helped to deliver copies to his subscribers.

In his *History of the Hastings Newspapers*, written in about 1903, Brett recalled:

> From the age of ten (after my father's sudden death [in 1826] with no provision for his family), I had laboured on an average of 18 hours a day, successfully – and sometimes coevally [simultaneously] – at domestic work, bakery, black-smithing, drapery, post office duties, tailoring, music and private teaching; also as band-master, dancing-master, pedagogue, amateur architect and corre-spondent of county newspapers. I had also in the course of that 29 years [before launching the *Gazette* in 1855] made myself acquainted with the mechanical pursuits of painting, glazing, carpentering, paper-hanging and even brick-laying. But before I started a newspaper, I knew nothing of printing.

Many a time Brett, with a Liberal perspective, was invited to stand for the town council, but he invariably refused, saying: 'I am too independent in politics, and too poor in pocket.' On his golden wedding anniversary in 1894 he was presented with an illuminated address and a sum of 200 guineas by his fellow townsmen. He died of old age on 4 April 1906, in his 90th year, at his Norman Road home.

Brett's Main Publications:

As Others See Us, *c.*1805 to 1830s, in two volumes.
Historico Biographies of Local Worthies, in five volumes. Written 1890–91.
History of St Leonards, 1828–1878. Written 1878.
History of the Hastings Newspapers. Written *c.*1893.
Manuscript History of Hastings and St Leonards, 1828 to 1864, in ten volumes. Written 1896+.
Premier Cinque Port, thirteenth century to *c.*1804, in four volumes.

These are all viewable on film in Hastings Reference Library.

The Archway, near where Brett lived, that marked the eastern boundary of Burton's St Leonards. It was demolished in 1895 because it was a 'traffic hazard'.

APPENDIX 5

THE ROCK FAIR

Three ancient fairs were held every year in Hastings, until they were brought to an end by the local establishment in the 1860s and '70s because of the 'trouble' they had been causing.

These fairs were combined funfairs, trading markets and social meeting places, where people could meet friends, conduct some business and have an enjoyable time eating, drinking, playing games and watching theatre shows.

The first annual fair on the calendar was the 'Whit-Tuesday Fair' at the end of May, which probably originated from pagan celebrations of the start of summer. The 'Winter Fair' or 'Town Fair' took place every 23 and 24 November. Both these fairs were held on the beach in front of the Old Town, the main site of the town of Hastings from the twelfth century, but the third annual fair, the 'Rock Fair', may have been even older.

The Rock Fair was held on 26 and 27 July every year, and in the nineteenth century (and possibly before then) was the biggest of the three fairs, with large numbers of all classes of people taking part. The reason for having it on those dates is unknown, but it may have been because by late July the annual mackerel-catching season would have ended, usually giving the fishermen some extra income that could be spent at the fair.

Victorian local historian Thomas Brett said that until 1822 the Rock Fair had always been held on the part of the America Ground where today Claremont, Trinity Street and

The Rock Fair in 1811. Today's Cambridge Road on the left.

Robertson Street form a triangle.[81] The 1827 government map of the Ground describes the Fair's location as 'Land formerly called Rock Fair Green'. The Green abutted the promontory of White Rock, the probable Saxon location of the town of Hastings, and it is most likely that the fair took its name from that headland.

In the early 1820s the Ground had started being heavily developed, and in 1822 much of the Rock Fair Green was taken over by the prominent Breeds family, forcing the annual Fair to find an alternative site.

The Fair was a very popular mixture of fun, games and social get-togethers, with many stalls supplying food, drink and games. It attracted large numbers of people from both the town and the surrounding countryside. But also by the early 1820s the Fair was becoming more problematic, as a Hastings man recalled: 'It resembled an ordinary fair, but a vast amount of gambling took place with halfpence, and fishermen often staked, and lost, their boats, nets and other appliances.'[82]

In 1823, having been forced to relocate, the Fair was held nearby, probably in a Priory Farm field, where Cambridge Road and Priory Street are now (Cambridge Road was then much lower, and one could walk on almost flat ground from Claremont through to the farm, which was where Cambridge Gardens is today).[83] This area was to become its main home in following years.

Commenting on the 1823 Fair, the *Sussex Weekly Advertiser* of 4 August 1823 reported:

> In consequence of the quantity of rain which had fallen, the intended spot for gaiety and ludicrous exhibition had a complete surface of mire and water yet the lads and lasses from town and country were not deterred from encountering all the difficulties and disasters arising from the inclemency of the weather, and boldly displayed their blooming, healthy countenance, robed in white gowns, and dashing coloured ribbons, best hats and holiday attire, wading through the scene of action, unaided by mud boots, and inundated with celestial dews, laughing at each other's bespattered appearance, and evidently enjoying the fun. Fortunately the fair terminated without any accidents, except a few discoloured eyes, and bruises, from pugilistic strifes.

The 1825 Fair had a 'very lively appearance … with numerous groups of fashionable visitants interspersed with country lads and lasses in their gayest clothing, and all was mirth and merriment'.[84] The 1831 Fair was 'extremely gay, and crowded with holiday folk, from the town and adjacent places'.[85]

The Fair Problems

By the mid-1830s the Fair was encouraging gambling and drunkenness on an increasing scale, but initially its real crime, as far as Hastings Council was concerned, was that local traders (heavily represented on the Council) suffered a serious loss of business while the Fair was taking place.

When the Government took possession of the America Ground in 1835 and removed all its occupants and buildings, the Council had an opportunity to redevelop the adjoining ground where the Fair was being held. As a result, the Council in 1836 considered building a harbour on the America Ground, and justified choosing that location in a statement: 'Having been formerly derelict and unenclosed, and served as a place for Hastings people to play at cricket and other games, and served for fishermen drying nets; that a public fair was held there from time immemorial; that no owner having asserted or maintained any claim to the land.'[86]

While drawing up plans for a harbour (which came to nothing), Hastings Council also set up a committee in 1837 to 'enquire into the circumstances of Rock Fair, with a view to it being abolished or to render it more useful and profitable to the town without interfering with rational amusements'.[87]

But this was also unsuccessful, and in 1846, as the Fair became increasingly rowdy, the Council tried to quash it altogether by issuing an official-looking notice saying that the Fair 'will cease to be held' because it was 'objectionable and of no public benefit'. Many local landowners also agreed not to allow it on their property. But the Rock Fair continued unabated, because by the mid-1840s Hastings had entered a period of sustained economic growth and expansion.

The local fishing industry was benefitting from the national railway network that was being built, as this opened up big new markets for their catches, and the Rock Fair was 'the fishermen's holiday, the only time in the year when all the fishermen put on their best clothes'.[88] In the mid-1840s it was even more popular than before, attracting large crowds of people of all ages to enjoy the 'medley of gingerbread nuts and dolls, Middleton [a theatre] and gypsies, peep-shows and penny trumpets, dwarves and giants, gangs and cheapjacks, drinking and dancing'.[89]

With better incomes, the fishermen and the other working-class people living in the boom towns of Hastings and St Leonards spent more of their new money at the Rock Fair on the proletarian pleasures of gambling and alcohol. But the large crowds of merrymakers were increasingly distasteful to the new generation of middle-class Victorian abstainers and shopkeepers.

Navigating the Navvies

The Council's problems with the Fair came to a head in the late 1840s when the Hastings area railway system was being built, and 3,000 hard-working and hard-drinking navvies moved into the town. The Fair had remained in the Priory Farm area for many years, but was forced to move out because of the siting of the railway station there. In 1850 the Fair was reported as moving onto the top of White Rock, between today's White Rock Gardens and Cambridge Road, part of Wastel Brisco's large estate.

The Fair was described as a 'grievous moral pest' by a letter writer in the *Hastings News* of 27 July 1849. 'Efforts have been made, both private and magisterial, to abolish it, and yet it lives.' The correspondent complained about the 'wholesale debaucheries, the disgraceful riots of every year's fair'. Another letter writer in that edition urged the authorities to clear the Fair before the evening of the following day, because that was the Saturday when the thousands of navvies were going to be paid their fortnightly wages.

The following year, 1850, the *News* reported that the Fair's 'especial patrons consisted of the most riotous and dissolute characters in the neighbourhood, the navvies forming a large proportion. The authorities withheld their countenance from the concern so that the parties who thought fit to visit the scene had it all to themselves. Fighting and drunkenness formed the substance of the proceedings.' It was just as bad in 1851: 'The amount of dissipation was quite sufficient to excite and to justify a desire that this excuse for riot and profligacy should be suppressed.'[90]

The 'annual saturnalia' of the Fair on White Rock in 1852 had constables in private clothes in attendance, on the lookout for gambling, which the mayor had ruled unlawful.[91]

The Abominable Fair

The navvies moved on from 1852, but the Fair remained a problem. It entered its last phase in 1858, when building work at White Rock and hostility from the owner of the ground, Wastel Brisco, forced it to move to farmland where Manor Road is today. This was part of Mount Pleasant Farm, owned by Henry Wyatt, a retired London brewer who had been in conflict with Hastings Council for trying to block footpaths on his extensive property.

Thomas Brett in the mid-1880s recalled that: 'The once famous annual festival, with its fancy stalls, fruit stalls, gingerbread stalls, oyster stalls, Middleton's marionettes, Richardson's theatricals, publican's booths, merry-go-rounds, glass-blowing and wax-works, together with giants, dwarfs and other monstrosities, was driven farther afield.'[92] Brett said that in 1858 'it was hoped that this degenerated Fair had died out for the want of a place to hold it'.[93] The *News* said: 'The Fair had gotten to be neither useful nor ornamental, but simply a rendezvous for the dissipated and vicious.'[94]

But the Fair lived on, and in July 1860 the local magistrates discussed 'this abomination', and whether it could be prosecuted for some offence relating to the sale of alcohol.[95] The law was unclear, however, so the Fair proceeded as usual that year. Twelve months later, in July 1861, the magistrates took a harder line, issuing a notice that all parties selling 'excisable liquors' at the 'illegal fair' would be prosecuted.[96] But the Fair promoters ignored the notice, claiming they had received the sanction of the excise authorities. That was not true, however, and after the Fair took place the Board of Inland Revenue threatened to take proceedings – but it was too late to find the offenders.

The Rock Fair's Obituary

The 1861 Rock Fair was reported as being a large event, but from then on it declined, and the last one of any size seems to have been held in 1864, when the borough magistrates posted a notice saying that the police would take action against all people selling excisable liquor there. There are no reports of it in later years.

In 1865 Mr Whyatt refused the use of his land for the Fair, probably because of the large amount of house-building then taking place in the Mount Pleasant area. So on 28 July 1865 the *Hastings News* published an obituary, saying that in the last few years there had been:

> a large increase of immorality in connection with it; and we wonder how anybody who knows how much drunkenness and debauchery have lately characterised this fair, can plead for its continuance on any ground whatever. The plea that the poor want amusement does not avail here; unless it be contended that such amusement should be sought in the company of the most abandoned of both sexes, and in the midst of the most revolting excesses.
>
> Very few of the respectable poor would be seen there; and of those who do go, the greater number have to rue it. We are glad then to learn that this fair has at last died out. … A visit to Rock Fair has cost many a man and woman the hard earnings of several days, and sometimes the character of a life.[97]

The Rock Fair in the early nineteenth century had been a wide-ranging, mainly working-class, social event and market, which the local establishment at that time felt able to patronise while the workers more or less behaved themselves. But as the town began rapid expansion in the late 1850s, and the Fair's market role declined, the Fair attracted many members of the increasingly vigorous labouring class who had come into the town to build the new houses and shops, and their 'bacchanalian' behaviour and culture conflicted with the increasingly abstemious attitudes of their employers and the local authority.

The End of the Town Fairs

Having quashed in 1864 the 'loathsome excrescence' known as the Rock Fair, Hastings Council turned its attention to the town's two other annual celebrations, the Whit-Tuesday Fair (also sometimes called the Whitsun Town Fair) and the November Town Fair. These very old social events had both been primarily for the fishermen, and like the Rock Fair, a key reason for them originally was as marketplaces, but this function was largely taken over by the increasing number of shops in the early Victorian years.

The traditional site of the two Fairs was at the bottom of High Street, where the small car park is today. In 1851 the November Town Fair 'comprised as usual a few gingerbread and peddlers' stalls', but on that occasion some seventy horses no longer needed for the works on the new railway were sold and gave the fair unusual importance.[98] But the Fair carried on declining, and in 1853 was described as 'a poor assembly of peddler's stalls and travelling shows'.[99]

Hastings Council began bringing to an end the two surviving Fairs by building a new retail fish market on their usual High Street site in 1870.

A petition was launched against the November Fair, and the editor of the *Hastings Observer* fully supported the campaign:

> Town Fair is an abominable nuisance to all respectable people in and about the neighbourhood, and a cause of dishonesty, drunkenness, and kindred vices and crimes in others. Children will steal, for boys and girls will dissipate their hard-won earnings on trash; men and women will get drunk over the glories of the Fair. For two days in every November the neighbourhood of the fish market is a perfect saturnalia with its shows and noise and bad characters.[100]

The last Whit-Tuesday Fair took place in late May 1871. The *Hastings News* said the Fair had 'nearly disappeared. This year it was only represented by about half a dozen small stalls for the sale of gingerbread and nuts.'[101]

Hastings Council voted in January 1872 to actually abolish both of the town fairs. Councillor Poole told the January Council meeting that 'he was sure the inhabitants – especially of that part of the town – would be very glad to have done away with what was an abominable nuisance; and to prevent the assemblage of a class of people who were no credit to the town or anybody else'.[102]

Both the town fairs had been established under the protection of a Royal Charter many centuries earlier, so the Council had to obtain the Secretary of State's consent, which was forthcoming in March 1872.

Ironically, in August that year, just five months after leading members of the Hastings establishment had finally managed to do away with the last of the town's ancient festive fairs, the powers-that-be themselves launched a new and even more popular form of mass entertainment, merriment and imbibing: Hastings Pier.

APPENDIX 6

PATRICK ROBERTSON

Patrick Francis Robertson (1807–85) was a wealthy Scottish entrepreneur who in the early 1850s turned the derelict America Ground into the town's main shopping street and seafront residential area. But the root of his wealth was opium. He had started making his fortune by selling opium to the people of China in the late 1820s and '30s, and then by benefiting from Britain's victory in the First Opium War of 1839–42.

Patrick was born on 24 August 1807 in Meigle, Perthshire, the eldest son of the Reverend Daniel Robertson (1755–1817) and Isabella Small (1774–1811). Daniel was Professor of Oriental Languages at the University of St Andrews in Fife from 1808 until he died in 1817. Isabella was a member of the Small family, owners of the Dirnanean estate near Meigle in Perthshire, and a branch of the Scottish Clan Murray of Atholl.

Isabella died when Patrick was 4, and he and his two younger siblings were raised by a maternal aunt, Cecilia Small. He obtained his formal education at the University of St Andrews.

Patrick paid his first visit to Hastings in 1824, about a year after leaving St Andrews. He probably came to visit his uncle Robert Small (1779–1850), Cecilia's brother, who had a residence in the town. This may have been what Robert, a London-based merchant, is known to have owned in the early 1840s: a former farmhouse and large estate, called Beaulieu, on the north side of the Ridge, where the Ark Helenswood Academy is today, opposite the Conquest Hospital.

Patrick Robertson.

To China

In 1826, at the age of just 19, Patrick sailed to Calcutta and joined uncle Robert's merchant company, Small, Colquhoun & Co., which traded between London, India and China.

Small's company was one of the agents of the all-powerful East India Company (EIC), which had a monopoly over British commerce with India and China. The EIC was set up in 1600, and by the eighteenth century was importing into Britain large amounts of spices, textiles and tea to meet the increasingly sophisticated demands of the rich class of people that was being created by the Industrial Revolution. Under Robert Clive (1725–74) the EIC became a powerful military force, taking direct control of much of India at the

Battle of Plassey in 1757. The company had become an imperial power, a profit-hungry corporation, run by shareholders, with its own private army to rule over millions.

With a single-minded pursuit of personal and corporate gain, the EIC and its executives achieved market dominance in much of the Far East, ruling over large swathes of India for a profit. But in China the country's rulers would only accept silver in payment for the teas, silks and porcelain that were so eagerly sought in Europe, and they would only do business through the port of Canton (now Guangzhou, China's third largest city, with 14.5 million people, the centre of southern China) on the Pearl River, about 75 miles upriver from Hong Kong.

Silver became expensive for the EIC to buy and use after the loss of America in the War of Independence 1775–83, but the company had access to a much cheaper commodity that was in great demand in China: opium. High in value and easy to ship, the opium poppy grew well in the EIC's hilly areas of India, where labour was also cheap. This powerful, dangerous drug had been illegal in China since 1729, but officials at the port of Canton were easily bribed to let it be smuggled in. From the 1780s the EIC grew high-quality opium extensively and cheaply, especially in Bengal, shipping it out through Calcutta, which became the capital of EIC's India. With the high profit margin on opium, the EIC could afford to pretend it was not an illegal smuggler itself by auctioning the opium, on the understanding that the independent purchasers of the opium would then smuggle it into China via Canton.

The illegal sale of opium became one of the world's most valuable single-commodity trades, providing 15 to 20 per cent of the British Empire's revenue.

Small, Colquhoun & Co. worked with the EIC, conveying goods between London, Calcutta and Canton. Patrick Robertson worked for them in Calcutta until 1831, when he moved to Canton to also work for a linked EIC agent, Turner & Co., for whom Small, Colquhoun & Co. were shipping agents. Patrick later became a partner in Turner & Co., which was owned by Richard Turner (1786–1839), who was a China resident from 1826, moving there from Calcutta. The book *The Taking of Hong Kong*, by Susanna Hoe, says Turner was 'one of the leading opium dealers (known as such to the Chinese authorities). Turner had traded in China waters since at least 1826.'

In 1833 the British government legally ended the EIC's trading monopolies in order to open up international commerce to other people. This resulted in the company's agents, such as Turner & Co., having a free hand to carry on their Chinese opium smuggling business more directly, and more profitably.

Opium balls stacked at the East India Company factory in Patna, Bengal, prior to shipment to Canton via Calcutta.

Following the ending of the EIC monopoly, in 1835 a mutual insurance society called the Union Insurance Society of Canton was set up to provide insurance for commercial cargoes using Canton. One of the original subscribers to this was Turner & Co., in which Patrick Robertson was then a partner.

The Opium War

The still-illegal opium trade through Canton expanded rapidly from 1834, seriously damaging the health of millions of Chinese people, and acting as a huge drain on the Chinese economy. Between 1821 and 1837 the importation of opium (theoretically a capital offence in China) increased fivefold.

In response the Chinese Emperor started an anti-opium crusade, appealing to Queen Victoria in 1837 to stop the traffic, but he was ignored. With foreign merchant vessels landing more than 30,000 of the 150lb chests of opium annually, the Emperor's campaign escalated. 'A hotbed of vice, bribery and disloyalty to the Emperor's authority, the opium port of Canton would be the flashpoint for the inevitable clash between the governments of China and Great Britain,' wrote Philip Allingham (see sources).

In early 1839 the Emperor's emissary to Canton, Lin-Ze-xu, seized 20,000 crates of opium in the port and held all foreign merchants under arrest until they surrendered opium worth $9 million, which he then burned publicly. This sparked the Opium War of 1839–41, which British naval and military forces won decisively. The Opium War, though named after a single substance, was fought over the cultural, diplomatic and trade differences between Britain and China.

At the end of the war, $9 million in reparations was given to the merchants – including Turner & Co. – whose opium had been burnt. To achieve peace, the Emperor had to sign

Chinese opium smokers. A picture by Thomas Allom, from *China Illustrated*, 1843.

treaties giving control of much of China's coast to the West, granting Britain most-favoured nation status for trade. Most significantly in the long run, China ceded to Britain the territory of Hong Kong, which was to become one of the most important ports in the Far East.

The company of Turner & Co. benefitted from the outcome of the First Opium War, but the business's owner, Richard Turner, died in March 1839, just as the war was starting. Later that year Patrick Robertson, who had lived in Canton through most of the 1830s and was a partner in the company, was appointed one of the executors of Turner's estate.

By the early 1840s Patrick had acquired considerable wealth, and he based himself in the UK, while continuing business enterprises in the Far East. Perhaps the most notable venture took place in June 1841. Britain had just taken over ownership of the island of Hong Kong at the end of the Opium War, and the government put up for sale fifty plots of key development land there, each with a 100ft sea frontage. Patrick bought the largest of these plots, with 35,000 sq ft of land, in what is now part of the heart of the city.

In June 1842 Patrick became part-owner of a large 637-ton square-rigged sailing ship, the *Robert Small*. She was built in 1835 for the Far East trade, and was named after Patrick's uncle. In 1842 Patrick took over 62-year-old Small's share of the vessel, which continued trading for many years.

Although Patrick was effectively living in Britain, from the early 1840s onwards he became involved in the management of several London-based international banking and insurances businesses, especially in the Far East. But he retained his connection with China: the 1851 national census described him as an 'East India and China merchant'.

In 1867, when Patrick was an MP, he was described in Debrett's guide to the House of Commons as being 'a sub-governor of the London Assurance Corporation (the world's first insurance company in 1710), deputy chairman of the Bank of Egypt, a director of the Oriental Bank Corporation and a merchant in the China trade'. He was also a director of the English and American Bank.

The Oriental Bank Corporation was established in 1842 in Bombay under the name of Bank of Western India. In 1845 the bank moved its headquarters to London and its name was changed to the Oriental Bank. In 1849 it took over the Bank of Ceylon, and in 1851 the bank was given a royal charter to operate anywhere east of the Cape of Good Hope, which immediately led to valuable expansion in many countries. Renamed in December 1851 as the Oriental Bank Corporation, it was primarily concerned with the finance of trade and exchanges of different currencies, becoming the largest exchange bank in Asia. In China, its priorities, along with conducting foreign exchange, were promoting opium trade and discounting long-term trade bills. According to Lloyd's, 'By 1860 it was one of the largest and most important British-owned banks, with assets of over £12.6m and 14 branches.'

To Hastings – and the America Ground

Patrick Robertson's uncle Robert Small, who had a house in York Terrace, Regent's Park, London, also had the Beaulieu estate on the Ridge in Hastings, which Patrick visited. About 1842 he decided to come and live in the town, probably initially staying at Beaulieu, until in 1847 he bought an attractive detached Hastings villa called Halton House. It stood in a large garden in Halton, where the eastern half of Hardwicke Road is today, overlooking Old London Road and the Old Town to the sea.

Patrick quickly became a well-known and popular local figure in Hastings. Historian Henry Cousins described him as 'a man of fine presence'. By 1847 he was also a prominent member of the local establishment, standing as a Liberal-oriented Conservative candidate for Hastings in that year's general election, although he was unsuccessful.

Through 1847 and 1848 it became clear that the national railway system would soon be arriving in Hastings, and Patrick could see that this would transform the borough. The siting of the main station in the Priory Valley would create a new town centre close to the empty America Ground, which the Crown had already made known was up for offers.

So in 1849 the wealthy international businessman – only 42 years old and with plenty of both spare time and money, following many years in the profitable opium trade – struck a deal with the Crown to rent most of the America Ground and carry out a large-scale development. This is described from page 94 onwards.

Robertson's Other Life in Hastings

After his major investment in the America Ground, Patrick carried out many political and social roles in Hastings, while continuing his worldwide business activities.

Following his death on 20 January 1885, the *Hastings News* obituary in its 23 January edition said:

> For some thirty years no gentleman was better known or more widely respected throughout the borough of Hastings than the subject of this notice. His hearty benevolence and genial nature made him the friend of all. Although constantly engaged in the fore-front of political warfare his personal qualities and kindly characteristics won the respect of his Liberal opponents. It was in the Chinese trade that he became affluent. Between 30 and 40 years ago he settled down at Hastings, at Halton House, where he resided with his sister and Miss Small.
>
> Mr Robertson was a supporter of every movement calculated to improve and benefit the local community. In his early days, before he lost a consider-able portion of his wealth from commercial collapse [of most Far East traders in the late 1860s/early '70s], he was ever to the fore in relieving the wants of his poorer brethren, and he was also in the true sense a leader of local society.
>
> His mansion and grounds at Halton have been the scene of some of the most fashionable garden parties, archery meetings, and other gatherings. At one period he was one of the most active supporters of the Hastings Mechanics' Institution, and on frequent occasions lent his beautiful grounds for fetes in aid of the funds. A Churchman of a decided type, Mr Robertson

was a regular attendant at Halton Church, and one of the chief support-
ers of Halton Parochial Schools. He was also a generous contributor to the
funds of religious societies, and showed particular interest in the local branch
of the Protestant Reformation Society, at the annual meetings of which he
frequently took the chair.

The Infirmary also had Mr Robertson's hearty support, and amongst other
institutions in which he took a practical interest should be mentioned the
local benefit societies. At Halton he built a Working Men's Club, and did
many other generous acts for the benefit of the working classes.

In 1879 the *Hastings Observer* of 11 January said that 'for 30 or more years' Patrick had
'been the honoured head of the Conservative Party of this borough'.

Patrick stood nine times as a Hastings candidate in parliamentary elections. In the
general election in August 1847 he was unsuccessful, but he was victorious in July 1852.
At that time Hastings had two MPs, and the other successful candidate in 1852 was
another Tory, Musgrave Brisco, a former mayor of Hastings in the 1830s, who was a
Hastings MP from 1844 until he resigned in 1854. Brisco was the brother of Wastel
Brisco Jnr, who had bought Bohemia House from the bankrupt Boykett Breeds in 1832.

Patrick served as an MP from 1852 until he was defeated by a Liberal in the April
1859 general election. He was again unsuccessful in the October 1864 election, but
was re-elected in July 1865. He stood down as MP in the late 1868 general election,
and was unsuccessful in both the 1869 by-election and the 1874 general election, after
which he did not stand again. He was also a Hastings JP for many years.

Patrick's life in Hastings from 1847 was centred on his home, Halton House, which
stood in a 6-acre estate off Old London Road, where Hardwicke Road and Rotherfield
Avenue are today. The estate was described in an advertisement in the *Hastings
Observer* of 23 June 1883 as having 'superior stabling, extensive lawns, terraced walks,
shrubberies and pleasure grounds'. The house contained '17 bed and dressing rooms,
five reception rooms, billiard room, conservatory and complete domestic offices. The
property contains all the advantages of a marine residence, with the seclusion of a com-
modious country house.'

The House was probably built in the early 1820s by a wealthy churchman, the
Reverend George Griffin Stonestreet (1782–1857). His father had founded the
Phoenix Assurance Company in 1782 and owned Standen Hall in Hertfordshire. The
Reverend himself was chaplain with the Guards at the 1815 Battle of Waterloo, and he
was prebendary of Lincoln in 1822–57.

Patrick was a lifelong bachelor, and after buying Halton House in 1847 his unmar-
ried sister Mary (1808–87) lived there with him. Uncle Robert Small's younger
daughter Cecilia (1815–74) also spent much time at Halton House, and Robert's
sisters Catherine and Ann stayed there.

Robert had died at Beaulieu in December 1850, and in the following years his house
was expanded and then replaced, probably in the early 1860s, with a bigger building, known as Beaulieu House. This in turn was replaced by a large mansion in 1883,
which itself in 1918 became a private boys' preparatory school known as Hydneye

Halton House, where the east end of Hardwicke Road is today. It was demolished in 1897. Barley Lane is in the distance, on the right.

House. The school closed in 1968 and in 1973 Hastings Council bought the attractive building and its large estate, but, in a highly controversial move, demolished it and built the existing school, Ark Helenswood Academy.

For two decades from 1847, the well-off Patrick had a good life at Halton House, living in some luxury while hosting numerous social and political events on his estate that both earned him many friends and helped the poorer people in the Halton area.

But his business interests in the Far East partly collapsed in the late 1860s, and from then on he had to lead a more frugal life. Attempts were made to sell the house, but these were unsuccessful, probably because the neighbouring impoverished working-class streets of Halton were not attractive to well-off house buyers.

The *Hastings Observer* on 26 May 1883 reported that Mr Robertson 'has been ill for some time past and has been removed to London. We also understand that Halton House and its contents will soon be brought under the hammer.' In early June the house contents were auctioned, and then later that month the estate and house were put on the market. They were sold in October 1883 to a local builder, Mr William Rogers of nearby Clive Vale.

Patrick died on 20 January 1885 in Hampstead, at the residence of his younger brother James, where he had been staying for about two years. He has a tomb in Hastings Cemetery.

After buying the estate, Rogers used the grounds for various events, but let the house fall into 'rack and ruin', as described by the *Hastings Observer* on 31 January 1891. He sold the estate and the unlet house in October 1894, and gave notice to quit to its caretaker, James White. Mr White, aged 79, found the situation so depressing that in early November he committed suicide by hanging himself from banisters in the house.

The new owner decided to try and build a housing estate, and in June 1895 Hastings Council gave planning permission for two roads: May Road (now called Rotherfield Avenue), and Evelyn Road (now Hardwicke Road), which connected

Hydneye House, on the Ridge.

with Halton Hill Road (now Robertson's Hill), with steps going down from Evelyn Road to Old London Road.

Halton House was demolished in the summer of 1897, and its building materials – bricks, tiles, slates, floorings, etc. – were sold by auction on 30 September. The many trees on the estate, including ash, elm, beech, chestnut and poplar, were then felled and sold that December. But no development took place,

Advertisement in the *Hastings Observer*, 23 June 1883.

and in November 1898 the estate was described as 'an unsightly wilderness'.

The estate – 'a desolate and dreary waste' – was finally bought by Mr G.T. Kellog-Jenkins in December 1900, and he obtained planning permission for 110 houses in October 1901.

The *Hastings Observer* of 22 December 1900 said that the houses would be low rent, and aimed at 'artisans'. They 'will be admirably suited for acquisition by artisans under clauses of the Housing of the Working Classes Act 1890 … and will be of great advantage to the working classes generally. It will, indeed form quite a model colony.' The roads approved in 1895 had been shaped and kerbed, and sewers laid when work began in late 1901. By mid-1902 houses were to let in the two new roads, Rotherfield Avenue and Hardwicke Road. They were the work of Henry Ward, the well-known local architect who had designed many prominent buildings in the town.

The small tightly terraced houses in Hardwicke Road were 8s 6d (42.5p today) a week, while the bigger, sea-facing homes in Rotherfield Avenue were £28 12s (£28.60) per annum.

The site of Halton House, at the east end of Hardwicke Road, lay empty until 1928, when 'slum clearance' started in the Old Town, the long-term project that ended with The Bourne being constructed through the Old Town in the early 1960s. The first Old Towners who were made homeless were rehoused in new council houses built where Halton House had stood, and are still there today.

Sources

There were many sources for this biography; these are the main ones.

Allingham, Philip V., *England and China: The Opium Wars 1839–60*. www.victorianweb.org/history/empire/opiumwars/opiumwars1.html

A People's History 1793–1844 from the Newspapers, Chaps 31, 34, 35. www.houghton.hk

Cousins, Henry, *Hastings of Bygone Days – and the Present*, 1920.

Dalrymple, William, *The Anarchy: The Relentless Rise of the East India Company*, 2019.

Debrett's Illustrated House of Commons, 1867.

Hastings News, 23 January 1885.

Hastings Observer, 11 January 1879 and 24 January 1885.

Lubbock, Basil, *The Opium Clippers*, 1933.

Mackenzie, Compton, *Realms of Silver: 100 Years of Banking in the East*, 2005.

McGuire, John, *The Rise and Fall of the Oriental Bank in the 19th Century*, 2004.

Oriental Bank Corporation archive, via Lloyd's Banking Group Archives.

Perdue, Peter C., *The First Opium War – The Anglo-Chinese War of 1839–42*, 2011.

Pichon, Alain Le, *China, Trade and Empire 1827–43*, 2006.

Portillo's Empire Journey, Transparent TV/Channel Five, 15 May 2020.

Robins, Nick, *The Corporation that Changed the World*, 2012.

The Chinese Repository, en.wikisource.org/wiki/The_Chinese_Repository.

Wikipedia entries:
    East India Company.
    First Opium War.
    Opium.
    Opium Wars.
    Oriental Bank Corporation.
    Patrick Francis Robertson.

Zhaojin Ji, *A History of Modern Shanghai Banking*, 2003.

APPENDIX 7

THE BRISCOS

The Hastings police station, courts, fire station, sports centre, cricket ground, ambulance station and Hastings Museum and Art Gallery are all standing on land that was once owned by a member of a rich slave-owning family.

The family was the Briscos, one of whom – Wastel Brisco Jnr (1792–1878) – in 1832 bought the Bohemia House mansion and its large estate on the east side of Bohemia Road from Boykett Breeds Jnr when he became bankrupt. Boykett Jnr and his family at that time also ran a large trading centre on the west side of Claremont, part of the America Ground, but they retained this despite Boykett Jnr's problems.

During the 1830s the Bohemia estate was extended to take in all the land on that side of the road, from Horntye down to White Rock Road, plus on the west side of Bohemia Road what are now White Rock Gardens and the Oval.

Wastel Jnr as a youngster, with his brother Musgrave Brisco Jnr (1791–1854), had owned a slave-run coffee plantation in southern Jamaica that his mother Sarah had inherited in 1798 from her aunt Jane Blinshall. Their Coffee Grove Plantation, which had seventy-five slaves in 1811, was sold in 1813, but the brothers maintained their affluent lifestyle, including the purchase of the Bohemia estate by Wastel Jnr.

This may have been partly thanks to his cousin, the wealthy Sir Wastel Brisco (1778–1862), who lived at Crofton Hall on a 780-acre estate in Cumberland, 6 miles south-west of Carlisle, which the Briscos had owned since 1390. The surname 'Brisco' is believed to have been derived from Birksceugh (meaning a birch wood), the original name of a small village (now called Brisco) a few miles east of Crofton Hall.

Sir Wastel owned 2,300 acres (7 per cent) of the island of St Kitts, one of the Leeward Islands in the Caribbean, where he had extensive sugar estates run by slaves. St Kitts was considered one of the most favourable islands for sugar production. He also owned Shadwell Great House on St Kitts, a still-surviving landmark that once served as the residence of the English governor of the island.

When the British government abolished slavery in August 1834, following the passing of the 1833 Slavery Abolition Act, the slave owners received compensation from the British state for the loss of their 'property' – the slaves. Sir Wastel was given £10,609 (more than £1.27 million in today's money) for losing his 651 slaves. The slaves received nothing. The government paid the hundreds of slave owners a total of £20 million, 40 per cent of the Treasury's annual income.

The brothers Wastel Jnr and Musgrave Jnr were part of the Hastings branch of the Briscos, one of the wealthiest families in the area. Musgrave Jnr played a prominent role in the town, being elected mayor in 1842, and MP from 1844 to 1854. From 1852 to 1854 his fellow Hastings MP was Patrick Robertson, lessee of the Crown's old America Ground.

The father of the two brothers was Wastel Brisco Snr (1754–1834), who owned Croft House, in the Croft, the largest house in Hastings Old Town. In 1792 he bought the extensive Filsham Farm estate in West St Leonards. Wastel Snr had a high-class residence in London, at 38 Devonshire Place, Marylebone, while Sir Wastel Brisco lived round the corner in elegant Wimpole Street. Wastel Snr was interred in St Clements Church, Hastings, after his death in January 1834, and the main heir to his fortune was Musgrave Jnr, being the eldest of several sons, who inherited 38 Devonshire Place.

Wastel Snr's parents were Musgrave Brisco Snr and Mary Dyne, daughter of Edward Dyne. Since at least the early seventeenth century the Dynes had owned and lived on the Lankhurst estate, covering many acres to the south-east of Westfield, including the Old Coghurst house and farm 3 miles north of Hastings.

In 1828 Musgrave Jnr married Frances Woodgate, and as a wedding present from his grandfather, it is believed they were given the Coghurst area of the Lankhurst estate, covering about 33 acres.

In 1830 Musgrave Jnr and Frances moved into the refurbished Old Coghurst house, the first record of which is from 1666. Then in 1834–35 he had the luxurious Coghurst Hall built on the estate, just to the west of the Old House. The designer of the grey stone mansion was Decimus Burton, the architect of the new town of St Leonards. A private driveway, almost a mile long, was made, with its entrance on the Ridge, where the Alsford Trade & DIY centre is today. A grand entrance lodge was built there in 1839, and demolished in the late 1950s. Musgrave Jnr died in 1854, and his wife Frances in 1867, after which Coghurst Hall passed to Wastel Jnr.

The hall was occupied by the Army in 1939. Most of it was demolished in 1952 and became the Coghurst Caravan Park. The now-100-acre estate is open 306 days a year, and consists of hundreds of large static caravans – for sale from £9,999.

Prior to moving into Bohemia House in 1832, Wastel Jnr, who received a liberal annual allowance from his father, had been living since at least 1824 at the Rose Green

Bohemia House, in its early days.

Mansion House on Battle Hill, opposite Battle Abbey. It was put up for sale by auction in June 1832, with an estate of about 350 acres of farmland in the Battle area, plus 56 acres of marshland at Barnhorn, near Bexhill.

The Brisco's Bohemia estate remained undeveloped when Hastings spread north and west during the nineteenth century, acting as a 'green lung' for the surrounding housing estates.

When Wastel Jnr died in April 1878 the *Hastings Observer* of 27 April reported that: 'He was a large landed proprietor, and was said to have been the wealthiest resident of these towns.' He had been chairman of the county magistrates for many years up until his death.

In April 1902 what is now White Rock Gardens was sold by the Brisco estate to Hastings Council for £20,000. The following year Bohemia House became a boys' prep school, and was renamed Summerfields House.

The house and other Brisco-owned property were put up for auction in the Castle Hotel by Major Arbuthnot Brisco on 20 April 1920. Some items did not reach the reserve price, but the house, its gardens and ten other lots of nearby property were sold, along with the 165-acre Filsham Farm and its 40-acre, nine-hole golf course. The house was bought by the tenant.

The widow of a wealthy doctor bought 2¾ acres of the Bohemia estate and in the early 1920s built a private house. This was later sold to Hastings Council, becoming Hastings Museum in 1927.

During the Second World War, Summerfields House was used as the town hall. It returned to use as a school after the war, closing as a school in August 1966, when the remaining 47 acres of the Brisco estate were purchased by Hastings Council for £170,000.

In 1968 the council began an ill-thought-out and chaotic development programme of the estate on the east side of Bohemia Road, hoping to create a 'civic centre complex', but instead patching together a shanty town of badly designed and unconnected buildings.

The first to be completed was the ambulance station, opening in June 1969, followed by the fire station in February 1971 and the police headquarters in July 1972. All are still there. The attractive Summerfields House, behind the fire station, was demolished in early 1973, and a collection of temporary planning offices were put there some years later.

The law courts opened in June 1975 and the long-delayed sports centre in August 1980. In May 1991 the first game of cricket was played on the Horntye cricket ground, which replaced the Central cricket ground.

In Hastings there are no Brisco statues or other obvious reminders of this once-prominent slave-owning family, apart from Brisco's Walk, running up the east side of the old estate, from Holmesdale Gardens to Horntye Road.

There is more Brisco information on https://bohemiabrisco.weebly.com/briscos-of-crofton.html.

APPENDIX 8

LISTED BUILDINGS

These are all the listed buildings on, or immediately adjacent to, the America Ground, as recorded on Historic England's website. Not all the history data on the website is correct; it has been rectified here as far as possible. Several historic buildings are not listed, including the old *Observer* building in Cambridge Road and the two early Victorian Buckingham Palace statues in front of Robertson Terrace.

The only Grade II* building is the Church of the Holy Trinity in Robertson Street/Trinity Street, built 1857–59.

Below are the Grade II buildings:

Brassey Institute, Claremont. Built 1878–80. Designed by W.L. Vernon for Thomas Brassey, MP for Hastings (created Lord Brassey 1886) in an eclectic Gothic revival style to house reference library on ground floor, assembly room on first floor, school of art and science on the upper floors, accommodation for the Hastings Rowing Club in the basement and a suite of rooms for the proprietor.

No. 14 Claremont. Built as a print works and shop for the *Hastings Observer*, as part of the Brassey Institute development.

1861 fountain on the corner of Robertson Street and Trinity Street.

United Reformed Church, on Robertson Street and Cambridge Road, built 1884–85. Designed by local architect Henry Ward. It is on the site of the Congregational Church, built 1857.

No. 21 Robertson Street. Shop built early 1850s, with 1924 unaltered Art Nouveau shopfront.

Former Memorial Photographic Studios, above 51 and 52 Robertson Street, on the corner of Cambridge Road. Purpose-built around 1864 for photographer F.R. Wells.

Havelock Pub, Robertson Street, backing onto Havelock Road. Built 1857, the year that General Havelock died after playing a prominent role in defeating the Indian Rebellion of that year. The bar was refitted in 1889–90 by Henry Ward, with murals by a Royal Doulton artist.

Nos 40–41 White Rock, plus the **lift shaft and winding mechanism** to the rear of the building, at Prospect Place. This was a carriage hoist for the showrooms and workshops of Rock and Sons, carriage manufacturers at 40-41 White Rock.

The 300m-long **Carlisle Parade underground car park**, the first underground car park in Britain. Included in the listing are the subway, the entrance ramps, the sunken garden and the three shelters. The roof of the garage is the A259 main road. Built in 1931, it was part of the large-scale redesign and rebuilding of Hastings seafront by the borough engineer Sidney Little that transformed the town.

APPENDIX 9

THE *HASTINGS OBSERVER*

The *Hastings Observer* at various times had four print works and offices close to what had previously been the America Ground: at Nos 12 and 14 Claremont; and at 53 Cambridge Road and its adjoining Rothermere House (now Rock House).

The *Observer* began life in 1853 as the *Rye Chronicle*, launched in Rye by local shop-keeper and printer Isaac Parsons, born in 1820. In 1855 the government scrapped the stamp tax on newspapers, which had made them expensive to buy, and this quickly led to a boost in the number of newspapers around the country. Parsons then experimented with publishing other papers in the Rye and Hastings area, including producing the short-lived *Hastings Times* from 34 High Street in Hastings.

The first newspaper to be called the *Hastings Observer* was set up in 1859–60 by Hastings printer Joseph Knight. He took over the Parsons print works in High Street when the *Hastings Times* folded, and managed to keep the *Observer* running until 1866.

Isaac Parsons, in the meantime, carried on publishing the *Rye Chronicle*, under various names, including the *Hastings and St Leonards Herald*. In 1863 he opened a new office and print works in Hastings at 21 Havelock Road, with his son Frederick James Parsons (1844–1900). In 1864 Isaac passed on the management of the Hastings premises to Frederick, then aged just 20.

It was Frederick who created the newspaper and its three buildings that we know today.

The *Hastings Observer* by 1866 had almost closed down, but Isaac Parsons then bought it from Knight, placing Frederick in charge. Later that year Frederick set up a business partnership with a 23-year-old Suffolk printer Henry Cousins, author many years later of *Hastings in Bygone Days* (see Bibliography).

Frederick and Cousins then merged the *Herald* with the *Observer* to become in 1867 the *Hastings and St Leonards Herald and Observer*. In 1873 this was relaunched as the *Hastings and St Leonards Observer*, as we know it today.

By the mid-1870s the *Observer* had become the town's leading newspaper. In Victorian years, most local newspapers had a political orientation, and the *Observer*'s was always pro-Tory. As the leader writer said at its 1873 relaunch: 'We are prepared to maintain and defend Conservative principles with all the vigour of the past.'

This pro-establishment bias remained a feature of the *Observer* and its parent company F.J. Parsons Ltd until the 1970s, and was to play a key role in shaping the history of the town. In Edwardian years, Robert Tressell wrote the highly influential pro-socialist novel *The Ragged Trousered Philanthropists*, which had Hastings and St Leonards as its setting. In it, Tressell renamed the *Hastings Observer* as the *Mugsborough Obscurer*. From the 1860s until the beginning of the twentieth century the *Observer* had strong opposition from pro-Liberal newspapers, but by Tressell's time, 1904–09, this had been almost wiped out.

Claremont

In late 1870 Parsons and Cousins moved to Claremont when they rented the first and second floors of a new building, 12 Claremont. Until then, the north end of Claremont had been the last surviving part of the Breeds family's America Ground general purpose yard, with other owners by *c.*1870. Local builder Henry Mills had constructed No. 12, and Parsons and Cousins sited their 'Steam Printing Works' there. The actual printing machinery may have been located in old sheds where the Library and No. 14 Claremont are today.

The Parsons and Cousins partnership ended in 1875, and Frederick then put together plans for a bigger print works in Claremont.

The creation of the new Parsons headquarters at No. 14 Claremont was part of a joint development project with the adjoining land, on which was to be built today's library. The Parsons family had acquired all this ground and Frederick sold the library site to the wealthy Thomas Brassey. Together, Frederick and Brassey commissioned the local architect Walter Vernon to create one high-quality building for their separate projects: the Brassey Institute and the *Observer* print works.

Brassey (1836–1918) was a respected public benefactor who acquired the Claremont site for his vision of a multi-purpose building that would help a wide range of people. The Institute was designed to facilitate both education and amusement, of the higher and better kind. The money that he was spending had been earned by his father, also called Thomas (1805–70). Thomas Snr had become heavily involved in the building of the British railway system from its first days, in the 1830s. In the 1840s he also took on major contracts abroad. At its height, his business was employing 100,000 people on a quarter of the globe. By the time of his death, he is said to have built 5 per cent of the world's total railway mileage.

Tory supporter Frederick Parsons and pro-Liberal Brassey may have had differing views on party politics, but they shared common interests as Freemasons, both being members of the oldest Hastings area lodge, the Derwent, founded in 1813, and this probably helped create their joint project.

Many images of printing were built into the frontage of No. 14, including in the middle a cast portrait of the famous pioneer printer William Caxton, with the date 1477 alongside. At the highest point of the building – a decorated arch above the top window – it says 'FJP 1877', while the foundation stone at the bottom next to the library has 'FJP 1876'.

In the following decades the Parsons company F.J. Parsons Ltd steadily expanded, especially in the run-up to the First World War, by which time the only rival paper was the Hastings edition of the *Brighton Evening Argus*. In 1914 Parsons bought the long-running *Sussex Express*, based in Lewes.

Cambridge Road

By 1914 the F.J. Parsons managers had realised that the business had expanded so much that more workspace and up-to-date machinery was urgently needed. No. 14 Claremont was too small, and it abutted a vertical rock face, with one or more caves in it possibly built by the Breeds family in the 1820s and '30s. Parsons already owned some of this area, having bought it with the site of No. 14 and the Brassey Institute in the mid-1870s.

Instead of moving elsewhere in the town, it was decided to buy the caves and the land on top of them, and build up from what is now the sub-basement of the *Observer* building. It is possible that the eastern half of the sub-basement was already a large cave, made by the Breeds family in the 1820s.

In 1914 the company acquired the buildings and former timber yard on the corner of Cambridge Road and Prospect Place, plus the houses Nos 1–4 Prospect Place, which all overlooked Claremont from a considerable height. Immediately after the war, a design for the new Parsons headquarters was drawn up by the well-known Hastings architect Henry Ward. He had designed the Hastings town hall (1880), the United Reformed Church in Cambridge Road (1884), Bexhill town hall (1908) and, at the end of his life, the Debenhams building in Robertson Street (1927).

Hastings Council gave planning permission for the Cambridge Road scheme in May 1920. Work had to start at Claremont level, where there may have been the large cave. Construction was so difficult that it had to be carried out slowly, a floor at a time. While this was under way, the Parsons expanded their business, which required much more floor space, and so in November 1922 Hastings Council gave permission for an extension up Prospect Place.

By the beginning of 1924 much of the complex six-floor, 40,000 sq ft building was ready for use, but it took until August that year to set up the machinery. The *Observer* issue of 18 October 1924 was the first to say it was printed at 53 Cambridge Road, which from then on was the company's address, although the building was not all fitted out until 1925.

No. 53 Cambridge Road was constructed throughout with reinforced concrete, and had a frontage of 52ft and a depth of about 150ft. The main entrance was on what was called the ground floor, with three floors above it. Below it were the two floors named as the basement and sub-basement.

In the sub-basement – at ground level in Claremont

Unloading newsprint outside the *Observer* office at 14 Claremont in early 1909.

– were the presses and the storage space for the large rolls of printing paper (newsprint). The Parsons company hired local unemployed people to hew out extensive caves and tunnels beneath the new building, stretching under Prospect Place towards Dorset Place. The basement – the next floor up – contained engines and dynamos for lighting and driving the works and rotary printing press.

On the ground floor of No. 53 when it was built were an elegant polished teak entrance and enquiry office fronting onto Cambridge Road, plus the general offices and letterpress machine department. On the first floor, the front of the building had the managerial offices and boardroom, while the rear portion contained the general composing department and the staff entrance, up Prospect Place. At the front of the second floor were the editorial offices of the newspapers and journals, while at the rear was the machine composing department. On the third floor were the bookbinding department, lithographic and offset printing and designing department, and half-tone block-making and photographic department.

A steel-framed seventh floor with a tin roof was added in 1954. Then in late 1959–60 a major extension was built, going further uphill in Prospect Place, replacing the houses Nos 5 and 6.

Similarly large-scale expansion took place a decade later, this time going down Cambridge Road. In the 1930s F.J. Parsons Ltd had bought all the premises between the *Observer* building and the Claremont steps, with plans being drawn up in early 1967 to replace them with a large office block. But this scheme was abandoned, and only Nos 49 and 51, adjoining the *Observer* build-ing, were demolished in the late 1960s, being replaced with the nine-storey Rothermere House. When this extension (now called Rock House) was completed in July 1970, the *Observer* described it as 'the nerve centre in the pro-duction of the *Hastings Observer*' and its other papers.

In early 1972 the Parsons family decided they could no longer carry on owning and running F.J. Parsons Ltd, and the business was sold to magazine publishers Morgan-Grampian Ltd, who only lasted until late 1973, then selling

Work under way on the 53 Cambridge Road building.

to Westminster Press. This followed the launch in September 1973 of the free independent paper, the *Hastings News*, whose non-establishment atmosphere attracted many readers and advertisers. This brought the *Observer*'s old-style monopoly to an end, prompting a succession of changes in ownership, and its eventual move out of 53 Cambridge Road in 1984 to Woods House in Telford Road, Hollington.

No. 53 Cambridge Road was both an extraordinary architectural feat and a folly – a huge investment in a tall, thin and curving building latched on to the edge of a sandstone cliff, the top of which is itself a steep slope. Because of the problems involved in converting this difficult structure to any other usage, No. 53 was only partly occupied for the first six years after 1984 and it then stood empty and unused from 1990. Between 1990 and early 2019 it had about thirteen owners and nearly as many planning permissions. All bar one of these owners made money on the property, but none carried out any repair.

In the summer of 2014 White Rock Neighbourhood Ventures acquired Rock House and converted it into a self-sustaining live/work space. Then in February 2019, Ventures bought the adjoining No. 53 and began a long-term project of large-scale restoration. Project champion Jess Steele said: 'As well as rescuing this beautiful building after years of dereliction, we want to provide life-changing opportunities for local people – both during the renovation an through long-term uses.'

A full history of the *Observer*, its buildings, and the other Hastings newspapers, up to 2007, is in the author's book *The Hastings Papers*; see Bibliography.

APPENDIX 10

KEY DATES

Ninth century: The town of Hastings came into being, probably centred on top of White Rock, with the valley between the West Hill and White Rock being a natural port.

*c.*1189–99: The Holy Trinity Priory, a small monastery, was built where Cambridge Crescent is today. The valley became known as the Priory Valley, and the Priory set up a large farm along the west side of the valley. The Priory left the town in 1417, but the farm remained in action, and was to play a role in the way the America Ground came into being.

Thirteenth century: The Priory Valley steadily silted up from this time onwards, with the town moving to the Bourne Valley, where the Old Town is today.

*c.*1580: In an attempt to revive Hastings as a port, some local business people received a large grant from Queen Elizabeth I to turn the Priory Valley into a type of harbour known as a haven. About half the grant was spent on building a sea defence embankment roughly where Cambridge Road is now, with the haven inland of it, but the project was never finished as the grant receivers disappeared with the rest of the money. But the embankment became the main roadway for people heading west along the coast from Hastings, and this was to form the inland (northern) boundary of the America Ground. The embankment stopped short of the West Hill, so the Priory Stream ran to the sea past the east end of it, where Harold Place is today, and this was to be the eastern boundary of the Ground. The embankment played a key role in the history of the town centre, as it hindered the drainage of the Priory Valley, which remained as simple farmland and marshes for the next two centuries. A bridge was built across the Priory Stream, which became the joining point of all the roads in today's town centre.

1780s: Hastings started to become a seaside resort, and the town began slowly spreading west under the Castle cliff.

1800: As the town expanded, the first major development took place on the America Ground (then commonly known as the Priory Ground). This was a large shipyard and ropewalk, erected by the Breeds family, who were the principal shipowners and merchants in Hastings in the late eighteenth and early nineteenth centuries. Their layout was to determine ways in which the Ground was built upon in the following years.

1810s: Hastings increased significantly in popularity as a resort, prompting expansion of the town towards its western boundary, the Priory Stream. But this growth needed many new building artisans and labourers, and so, with a shortage of spare land in the town, an increasing number of people moved onto the Ground, some living there, others running their own businesses.

*c.*1820: Hastings had become a 'boom town', with large-scale development taking place between the Old Town and the Priory Stream. But it seemed that no particular person or organisation owned the Ground, and Hastings Corporation was not exercising any control over it, and as a result many of the occupants were squatters. The marshes on the north side of the *c.*1580 embankment were too wet to build on.

1821: Most of the Ground was shingle that had accumulated against the *c.*1580 embankment, and as the Crown owned all foreshore – i.e. land between high and low water marks – did the Crown own the Ground? A survey was carried out to examine the emerging problem, although no action was taken as a result.

1821: The wooden bridge across the Priory Stream was washed away in a storm, so a bigger bridge made of brick and stone was built. This was to be the site of the Albert Memorial clock tower erected in 1863.

1822: The Breeds family bought some of White Rock, between today's Prospect Place and Claremont. They cut back the hillside to create today's The Alley, and built a large trading centre, taking up all of the west side of Claremont.

1826: Squabbling between the Ground's occupants over landownership prompted the Crown to start legal action.

1827, 6 December: A government-organised 'inquisition' took place at the George Inn in Battle, which decided that the Crown owned all the Ground, apart from only half of the Breeds' centre in Claremont, as the other half of that was not standing on shingle.

1828 May: The Crown gave a seven-year notice to quit to all the Ground's occupants, apart from the Breeds in Claremont.

1829: A survey of the 8½ acres of the Ground by the Crown, published in 1830, found there were more than fifty industrial-type buildings, plus over 150 'residences'. The 1831 national census recorded 1,074 people living in the Holy Trinity Parish, nearly all of whom would have been on the Ground. A third of the Ground was occupied by the Breeds family.

1832, 19 July: A huge banquet was held on the Priory Brooks (where the Priory Meadow shopping centre is today) in celebration of the passing of the parliamentary Reform Bill. This is the only recorded occasion when the American Stars and Stripes flag was flown on the Ground. Hastings Corporation allowed an amended version of the flag to be displayed, and after the day's events it was presented to the town hall.

1835 December: This was the date by which all the Ground's occupants had to leave – and they had.

1836: The 'Priory Ground' became known as the 'Crown Land'. The name 'America Ground' appears not to have come into common use until the late 1840s.

1837–38: The Crown erected a stone wall along the edge of their land to protect it from the sea. The White Rock headland had been cut back in recent years, allowing the construction of a better seafront road to the new town of St Leonards, but thereby exposing the Crown Land to damage by gales.

1838: Cambridge Road as we know it today was built as a turnpike road, slightly to the north of the old road, which had been on the c.1580 embankment. This meant that the Crown Land did not include the west side of the new Cambridge Road.

1839: The bridge over the Priory Stream was replaced by a culvert where Harold Place is today. The area on and around the culvert was surfaced and levelled, creating the open space that became the heart of the town from the 1850s.

1846 July: The first train arrived in the town, at a temporary station at Bulverhythe. Over the next five years, many tunnels and three different railway lines were built, centred on Hastings Station close to the Crown Land.

1849: Wealthy Scottish businessman Patrick Robertson signed a deal with the Crown for a ninety-nine-year lease of the Crown Land for £500 pa. He realised that the arrival of the railways in Hastings would turn the Priory Valley into a new town centre, so he embarked on transforming the former America Ground into a high-quality residential and shopping district.

1850, 24 June: Work began on Robertsons's Ground with the laying of the first stone of the western part of Carlisle Parade.

1850, 4 October: The first shop opened – Mr Henry Polhill's pork butchery at 4 Robertson Street, where the HSBC bank is today.

1857, 22 July: The foundation stone of the Holy Trinity Church in Robertson Street was laid.

1877–78: The Brassey Institute (today's Library) and a new print works for the *Hastings Observer* were built as a joint project in Claremont.

1927: The Plummer Roddis department store was built, later becoming Debenhams, which closed in May 2021.

1931: The biggest change to Robertson's Crown Land was the reclamation of a further 60ft of the foreshore to create Britain's first underground car park, and to lay on top of it today's A259 main road. Inside the car park, the inland wall is the 1837–38 sea defence wall.

NOTES

For more details of references to the publications below, see the Bibliography.

Baines	Baines's Historic Hastings
Brett, Manuscript	Brett's Manuscript History of Hastings and St Leonards; see Appendix Four
Brett, Historico	Brett's Historico Biographies of Local Worthies; see Appendix Four
ESRO	East Sussex Record Office
Funnell	Funnell's The America Ground
Chronicle	Hastings Chronicle (newspaper)
Horsfield	The History, Antiquities and Topography of Sussex
News	Hastings News (newspaper)
Observer	Hastings Observer (newspaper)
SWA	Sussex Weekly Advertiser (newspaper)
SAC	Sussex Archaeological Collection

1 SAC, vol. 14 p.84.
2 SAC, vol. 14 p.90.
3 Archaeological Evaluation of the Cricket Ground, 1995, p.7.
4 *Hastings Guide*, 1794, p.55.
5 Baines, p.201.
6 Baines, Chap. 26.
7 Horsfield, p.448.
8 Banks, p.67.
9 SWA, 24 March 1806.
10 *Eliza Cook's Journal*, vol. 5, April–October 1851, p.333.
11 SWA, 7 August 1815.
12 SWA, 30 October 1820.
13 Funnell, p.5.
14 Brett, *Historico Biographies of Local Worthies*, vol. 1 p.77.
15 Brett, *Historico*, vol. 2 p.135.
16 Brett, *Manuscript History of Hastings and St Leonards*, vol. 6 p.41.
17 SWA, 17 March 1823, and Brett, *Manuscript*, vol. 2 p.123.
18 Brett, *Manuscript*, vol. 2 p.226.
19 Brett, *Manuscript*, vol. 2 p.226.
20 *Brighton Guardian*, 19 June 1828.
21 SWA, 18 August 1823.
22 Brett, *Historico*, vol. 1 p.70.
23 SWA, 3 September 1827.
24 Brett, *Historico*, vol. 2 p.180.
25 *Observer*, 9 Dec 1899.
26 Brett, *Manuscript*, vol. 2 pp.149–151.
27 Brett, *Manuscript*, vol. 3 p.296.
28 Brett, *Manuscript*, vol. 3 p.288.
29 Hastings Pavements Minute Book A, 5 April 1824.
30 Brett, *Historico*, vol. 1 p.24.
31 Brett, *Manuscript*, vol. 3 p.254, and *Historico*, vol. 1 p.24.
32 SWA, 31 August 1829.
33 Peak, *Fishermen of Hastings*.
34 *Brighton Guardian*, 19 June 1828.
35 Hyde, p.13.
36 Brett, *Manuscript*, vol. 1 p.13.
37 Commissioners' Sixth Report, Appendix A.
38 SWA, 10 December 1827.
39 Brett, *Manuscript*, vol. 1 p.13.
40 Peak, *Fishermen of Hastings*
41 ESRO MIL 3/2/28.
42 Brett, *Manuscript*, vol. 1 p.5.

43 Commissioners' Sixth Report.

44 Commissioners' Seventh Report.

45 *Sussex Express*, 3 Aug 1861.

46 Brett, Manuscript, vol. 1 p.24.

47 Report of the Commissioners on the Poor Laws, 1834, vol. XXVIII p.197a.

48 Brett, *Manuscript,* vol. 1 p.60.

49 Brett, *Historico*, vol. 1 p.33.

50 Brett, *Manuscript,* vol. 1 p.117.

51 Brett, *Manuscript*, vol. 2 p.124.

52 Brett, *Manuscript*, vol. 2 p.148.

53 Funnell, p.9.

54 Brett, *Manuscript*, vol. 1 p.115.

55 Brett, *Manuscript*, vol. 2 p.134.

56 Municipal Corporation Boundaries Report 1835, p.999.

57 Report from Hastings Council to Commissioners, 28 May 1836. In ESRO ref DH/B/182/580.

58 ESRO, ref DH/C/3/1/D35/17.

59 Hastings Town Records vol. 14, 11 June 1836.

60 Hastings Town Records vol. 14, 9 November 1838.

61 Baines, p.150.

62 Brett, *Manuscript*, vol. 2 p.226.

63 *Brighton Gazette*, 12 November 1840.

64 *News*, 12 May 1848.

65 ESRO, ref DH/B/185/5.

66 *Chronicle*, 2 January 1849.

67 Brett, *Manuscript*, vol. 3 p.332.

68 *News*, 15 Feb 1850.

69 *News,* 15 Feb 1850.

70 SWA, 19 February 1850.

71 Brett, *Manuscript*, vol. 4 p.191.

72 *News*, 1 August 1851.

73 Funnell, p.13.

74 SWA, 4 July 1854.

75 SWA, 16 May 1854.

76 Brett, *Manuscript*, vol. 5 p.211.

77 Leachman, Chap. 2.

78 *Observer*, 1 Jan 1910.

79 *Observer*, 1 Oct 1927.

80 Brett, *Manuscript*, vol. 2 p.124.

81 Brett, *Manuscript*, vol. 14 p.53.

82 SAC, vol. XXXIII p.247.

83 Brett, *Manuscript*, vol. 3 p.288.

84 SWA, 1 August 1825.

85 SWA, 8 August 1831.

86 Brett, *Manuscrip*t, vol. 2 p.138.

87 Brett, *Manuscript*, vol. 2 p.189.

88 *News*, 27 July 1855.

89 *News*, 1 August 1856.

90 *News*, 1 August 1851.

91 *News*, 30 July 1852.

92 Brett, *Historico*, vol. 2 p.158.

93 Brett, *Manuscript*, vol. 7 pp.78–9.

94 *News*, 23 July 1858.

95 *News*, 27 July 1860.

96 *Chronicle*, 31 July 1861.

97 *News*, 28 July 1865.

98 *News*, 28 November 1851.

99 *News*, 25 November 1853.

100 *Observer*, 2 December 1871.

101 *News*, 2 June 1871.

102 *News*, 12 January 1872.

BIBLIOGRAPHY

This book has drawn as much as possible on contemporary nineteenth-century sources, which are listed below along with more recent useful publications.

There are many websites and Facebook pages with material on Hastings and St Leonards. Try the author's *www.HastingsChronicle.net*, the late Ion Castro's *www.1066.net*, plus *wikipedia.org/wiki/Hastings*, Hastings Council's *www.hastings.gov.uk* and *wiki.historymap.info*.

Adams's Illustrated Descriptive Guide to the Watering Places of England, 1848.
Arundale's Pictorial Guide to Hastings and St Leonards, 1842. Revised and republished as *Hope's Pictorial Guide* in 1849.
Baines, John Manwaring, *Historic Hastings*, 3rd edition, 1986.
Banks, John, *Reminiscences of Smugglers and Smuggling*, 1873.
Barry, James, *The Hastings Guide*, 1797, 1804, 1815, 1817. These were revised editions of Stell's 1794 book – see his entry below.
Brett, Thomas Brandon, See Appendix 4.
Cole, Thomas, *The Antiquities of Hastings*, 2nd edition, 1884.
Commissioners of Woods, Forests and Land Revenues, Sixth Report, 5 June 1829, Parliamentary Papers 1829 XIV; Seventh Report, 8 June 1830, Parliamentary Papers 1830 XVI.
Cousins, Henry, *Hastings of Bygone Days*, 1911 and 1920.
Crux, Alex, *A Ramble about Hastings and St Leonards*, 1848.
Diplock's Handbook for Hastings, 1845.
Diplock's New Guide to Hastings, c.1849.
Diplock's Hastings Past and Present, 1855. This was significantly expanded and republished in 1864 as *Diplock's Handbook for Hastings*, with later editions.
Funnell, Barry, *The America Ground*, 2nd edition, 1989.
Horsfield, Thomas Walker, *The History, Antiquities and Topography of Sussex*, 1835.
Hastings Area Local Studies Project, *How the Railways Came to Hastings*, 1984.
Hyde, Anthony, *The Breeds of Hastings*, 2nd edition, 2014. Plus notes of lecture by Mr Hyde in April 2015.
Leachman, E.W., *A Church on No Man's Land*, 1934.
Local Newspapers, viewable on film at Hastings Library:
Cinque Ports Chronicle 1838–41.
Hastings and Cinque Ports Iris 1830–31.
Hastings News 1848–1905.
Hastings Observer 1853 to date.
Hastings and St Leonards Gazette 1855–96.
Sussex (Agricultural) Express 1837 to date.
Sussex (Weekly) Advertiser 1745–1904.
Martin, David, 'Hastings Augustinian Priory – An Excavation Report'. Hastings Area Archaeological Papers No. 2, 1973.

Moss, William G., *The History and Antiquities of the Town and Port of Hastings*, 1824.

Osborne's Strangers Guide to Hastings and St Leonards, 1853.

Parson's Guide to Hastings and St Leonards, 1st edition, 1876, plus several others till 1890.

Peak, Steve, *Fishermen of Hastings*, 2nd edition, 2005.

Peak, Steve, *The Hastings Papers*, 2007.

Pelham Arcade Library, *Hastings and St Leonards Guide*, October 1828. The first guidebook to include St Leonards.

Powell, P., *Guide to the Lodging Houses of Hastings*, 1819.

Ross's Hastings and St Leonards Guide, 1835 onwards in many editions, to *c.*1864.

Southall, C.H., *Southall's Pocket Guide to St Leonards and Hastings*, *c.*1838.

Stell, John, *The Hastings Guide*, 1794. The first Hastings guide book, taken over and republished in 1797 by James Barry – see his entry above.

Swarbrooke, Chris, *The America Ground and the Birth of Robertson Street*, date unknown.

Wooll, George, *Wooll's Stranger's Guide to Hastings and St Leonards*, 1833.

INDEX

The name 'America Ground' (often shortened to 'Ground') appears so frequently in this book that it is not listed here. The origins of the title are explained on pages 14, 41, 82 and 114. The names of the members of the Breeds family – Boykett Snr, Boykett Jnr, James, Mark and Thomas – also occur on so many pages that to try and index them separately would be confusing, so they are all listed under 'Breeds family' below. A family description starts on page 31.

Appendix 3 'The America People' has all the people named in the 1829 Crown survey, plus others connected with the Ground.

The destination for history
www.thehistorypress.co.uk